*Gourmet Cooking
for Vegetarians*

Colin Spencer

Gourmet Cooking
for Vegetarians

Robin Clark

For Brigid and Maureen
with love and thanks

Published by Robin Clark Limited 1980
A member of the Namara Group
27/29 Goodge Street, London W1P 1FD
Reprinted 1983, 1985

First published in Great Britain
in hardcover by André Deutsch Limited 1978

Made and printed in Great Britain by
Hazell Watson & Viney Ltd, Aylesbury, Bucks
ISBN 0 86072 035 7

Contents

Preface

Good vegetarian cooking has a tradition older than that of French *haute cuisine*. It goes back to the ancient civilizations of the Middle and Far East; it is not mere accident that where the creative arts have flourished there has also been a tradition of imaginative cooking, a respect for food and certain ritual manners of eating. Yet most vegetarian cookery books inflict upon a diet of vegetables a dour aspect. The mere thought of a nut rissole brings on a drought in the salivary glands. What could be more depressing than those various brands of nut pastes, said to resemble liver *pâtés*, nestling on the shelves of health food shops or those countless recipes calling for spoonfuls of Marmite, Yeastrel or Barmene on the grounds that they provide Vitamin B and strengthen the flavour of savoury dishes?* Vitamin charts demolish the first claim and, as to the second, my palate boggles! Why mask, confuse and ruin the huge range of delicate flavours to be found in vegetables? The finest cooking is and always has been that which gently brings out the intrinsic nature of the food being prepared. Seasoning should stimulate the food's own flavour by fusing with it or be used as a delicate grace note of dissonance.

Gourmet cooking is based upon a respect for food. Not only should you appreciate and enjoy the true flavour of the food you are cooking, but also understand, instinctively at least, its chemical structure. Then you will know, for instance, when the application of heat is beginning to break down a food too far and to halt a process (see page 81 on boiling eggs). Far too many vegetarian recipes give boiling times that amount to mass slaughter. The truth is that few vegetables ever need to touch water, save for a brief washing. All those with a high water content – leeks, spinach, endive, lettuce, chicory,

* It is only Vegans who need worry about the Vitamin B complex; dairy produce and yeast are rich in it.

cabbage, sprouts, broccoli, cauliflower and spring greens – can be poached gently for a few minutes in butter or olive oil. The liquor they lose can be made into a sauce or kept for soup, and nothing need be wasted. With the right type of pan (see Kitchen Equipment), vegetables can be cooked without even the addition of butter or oil, according to the methods of *la cuisine minceur* publicized recently by Michel Guérard.

The shortcomings of most vegetarian cookery books are explained, I believe, by vegetarians feeling that they ought to apologize for their habits. Such concoctions as nut roasts, rissoles etc. make a deferential gesture in the direction of the meat course. There is, in fact, no reason why anyone should feel shy about choosing a meatless diet, whether purely as a matter of taste or for moral reasons.

My reasons for preferring vegetarian cookery are two. First, I like vegetables more than I like meat (and the more I cook them, the more I enjoy their immense variety). Second, now that the world is threatened by famine and dietary diseases, we must face the fact that our eating habits will have to change. Feeding up vast quantities of cattle in order to eat them is a wildly extravagant way of using what the earth can produce. If the land used for this purpose was devoted to the production of cereals, we could banish the spectre of world famine. The beef-eaters of the affluent West are the worst offenders. Pigs can be kept in pens and fed on scraps, and sheep can be grazed on moors and mountains. However, the bovine family has to occupy land that could produce, plentifully and cheaply, food which could go directly into people's stomachs, instead of making its way there, indirectly and expensively, in the form of beef. I see this as the most important reason for rescuing vegetables from the bondage of earnest food faddists and proving that a vegetarian diet can be far from austere or boring. Approach it with the respect and imagination that has traditionally been devoted to *haute cuisine*, and *haute cuisine* is what you will have.

The methods used in this book come from three sources, by way of my own taste and experience: the Middle East, France and China. Chinese methods of preparation and cooking are the best of all for retaining the flavour of vegetables, although contemporary Chinese restaurant cooking has been somewhat polluted by modern short cuts, such as the reliance on tinned and frozen vegetables and on monosodium glutamate.*

Tinned and frozen vegetables may be just as nourishing as fresh ones, for all I know, but very few of them taste anything like the original, and if you try to extract their water content for a sauce or a soup, the result is lamentable. Fresh vegetables cost less, and almost every bit can be utilized. People's palates and minds are so easily conditioned by habit, that many think the taste of the frozen pea is the *right* taste for peas to have. I recommend frozen broad beans in one recipe and tinned artichoke hearts in another, but usually I have avoided contributing to what seems to me a tragic perversion of taste.

There are plenty of main-course recipes in this book, but on the whole the collection reflects my distinct preference for small dishes to pick and choose from, rather than one plate piled high with everything. Mine is the classic Chinese style of eating, and it lends itself to the proper awareness of each flavour and texture. It is also a manner of eating which fits in well with good conversation – and that, after all, is what a gourmet meal is for. It should be a celebration which releases pleasure and stimulates social communication.

I have tried to destroy a few myths; for example, in the section on garlic that ends the book. I have suggested some remedies for an unfortunate side-effect produced by the delicious family of pulses: their tendency to produce flatulence. Above all, I have attempted to prove that vegetables are worthy of the sensitive understanding given by the great French chefs to a *soufflé*, a *brandade* or a galantine. For this reason, I believe the book to be for non-vegetarians who enjoy good food as much as for vegetarians. There are so many ways of cooking vegetables with style, without losing their goodness and flavour; they can provide myriad delicate and delicious dishes. Even those who feel deprived unless they have meat every day will eat more enjoyably if they take vegetables seriously.

---

* 'Glutinous sodomites', as a friend of mine, a Dutch sculptress, calls it. Although meant to enhance flavour, it really adds another. With some people, it can be slightly addictive, and a few are violently allergic to it.

Points to Remember

1 Vegetables that grow above ground have a high water content. When cooking them, it is illogical to add more water, thus diluting the flavour and often wasting the goodness.

2 Forget the cooking times most of us were brought up to believe in. They are too long in almost every cookery book I know; the proper time can be a matter of seconds. If a vegetable is ruined in two minutes, then two minutes is too long. Start by testing and tasting your vegetables almost as soon as they begin to cook. You may well be amazed by how soon they are done.

3 When flavouring with herbs or spices, or mixing with *sauce vinaigrette*, toss the vegetables in the flavouring immediately after cooking, while they are still hot. Hot into cold fuses the flavours.

4 Use fresh herbs whenever you can. If you can grow them in your garden, so much the better. Packaged dried herbs have often lost their character even before you buy them, and anyway will do so quickly in your kitchen. When I have to rely on dried herbs, I find the ones I use most are bay leaves, thyme, oregano, rosemary, marjoram and sage. Dried parsley, mint and chives are useless – one might as well use chopped grass and wood ash. Keep dried herbs in light-proof containers and be ruthless about replacing them as soon as they lose their characteristic smell.

5 Grind spices yourself with a small pestle and mortar, because they too will have lost their virtue if ground and then packaged. Grinding takes only a few moments. Light-proof containers are the best, as for herbs.

6 Slicing. Root vegetables should usually be sliced diagonally, in the Chinese manner, because it exposes the largest possible area to cooking. Oddly, the only vegetable the English cut this way is the runner bean, which I prefer to trim and leave whole. Sometimes, of course, a recipe demands cubing, mincing or whatever, but slice on the bias when you can. Soft vegetables should usually be sliced along their natural

shape. For example, slice leeks lengthways in millimetre strands, which will cook in moments. Whether you slice lengthways or across should be dictated by the nature of the vegetable: the round radish looks better in discs, the peppery Mediterranean one in *julienne* strips. It is not just a matter of aesthetics, but also of shortening the cooking time, whether the vegetable is hard or soft.

7 Oil. I think that olive oil is unquestionably the best. It is very expensive now, but look what you are saving by eating no meat or by cutting down on it. The blacker and less refined the oil is, the more I like it, but this is a matter of taste. Certainly blended olive oil is often inferior. Vegetable or sunflower oils can be used for the highly spiced dishes either as an ingredient or when cooking, for in those the olive flavour is not needed. Oil, too, keeps its virtue longer if protected from light.

8 Seasoning. To me, this means sea salt and black (or a mixture of black and white) peppercorns, which you grind in a pepper mill. Seasoning is usually best added after the vegetable is cooked and before the sauce is made.

9 Mustard. *Moutarde de Meaux*, made by Pommery, quotes Brillat-Savarin on its label: 'If it isn't *Meaux*, it isn't Mustard'. I agree with him. Get it if you can (I know that Fortnum and Mason, Jacksons of Piccadilly, Harrods, Selfridges and many of the best delicatessens stock it). It must be tightly sealed after use, or it will lose its strength.

Measurements

A cookery-book writer gives measurements because a cook must start from some fairly strict basis, but no one has to be pious in following them. Taste, appetite, utensils, ovens – they all vary. How large is 'a small onion'? Is a recipe 'for four' enough when they are all ravenous? I give weights in both ounces and grammes, and expect you to adjust them if you wish. The recommended spoonfuls should also be subject to your individual taste, even more so the 'handfuls' of herbs. Sniffing and tasting are much more important than strict adherence to measurements. If the food tastes right, then you haven't gone wrong, so keep a constant check on the flavour of any dish you are cooking.

Kitchen Equipment

Here is my list of the tools essential to preparing good meals, with a few luxuries thrown in for those who can afford them.

1 At least three saucepans with thick bottoms and tight lids. Enamelled cast-iron ones are good, and so are those in stainless steel with a cast-aluminium bottom. Don't try to economize on saucepans. The thick bottoms stop burning and the really tight lids prevent the vital steam from escaping.

2 A *tian*. This shallow earthenware dish is something I use almost every day, and ideally one should have three or four of them in different sizes. *Sautéed* or poached vegetables can be placed in them with the sauce poured over. Then the *tian* can go into the oven or under the grill and from there on to the table. The earthenware keeps the food hot, no lid is needed, and you can dispense with vegetable dishes.

3 A large *marmite* for the slow cooking of pulses in the oven. One can get them in enamelled cast iron, but I prefer earthenware.

4 A set of ramekins. These little individual *soufflé* dishes are indispensable for many things besides *oeufs en cocotte* or *oeufs mollets*.

5 A heavy, enamelled, cast-iron frying pan (or a copper one, if you can afford it, keeps the heat better). This is essential for Chinese cooking, although a wok, with its wok-ring, simplifies the cooking and will easily give you the most authentic results.

6 A double saucepan is useful for steaming, though I would not bother to buy a *bain-marie*, which can always be improvised.

7 A thick wooden chopping block.

8 Good knives. A set of carbon steel ones and at least one of stainless steel, because some vegetables react harshly to carbon steel.

9 Several pudding basins of different sizes, for the mixing and fusing of flavours.

10 A set of wooden spoons.

11 A small pestle and mortar for grinding spices and crushing herbs. This can also be done by putting the herbs or spices between sheets of greaseproof paper on the chopping block and attacking them with a wooden mallet, a rolling pin or a milk bottle used like a rolling pin.

It is also necessary to have a colander, a pepper mill, a perforated spoon, a spatula, a wire whisk, a bread tin and a grater that stands securely on the table. A *mandoline* is not essential, but it does make the preparation of *gratin* dishes easier. A *mouli-julienne*, which can still be bought at reasonable cost, is also a marvellous asset when vegetables need to be sliced small.

Luxuries. All sauces and *purées* can be made with the above, but an electric blender makes life easier. I find a four-bladed blender the most satisfactory. A coffee grinder kept for the sole purpose of pulverizing the more obstinate spices is a help when you are making curry powder.

Basic Stores

You can prepare a dozen dishes at a moment's notice if your kitchen is stocked with the following: onions, carrots, garlic, lemons, enough flour to make a loaf and a *roux* for a sauce, a dozen eggs, milk, a pound of cooking cheese, a selection of pulses, butter, olive oil and a range of herbs and spices. A stock of rice and/or pasta is also useful, with a few tins of tomatoes and tomato *purée*. It is cheaper to buy the *purée* in big tins, which once opened will keep for some weeks in the refrigerator if you cover the contents with a layer of olive oil.

If you are a cautious user of herbs and spices, do not stock up with too many because they will just go dry and musty. Try, though, to become more adventurous with them. I find it sad that we are so conservative, considering how freely we used herbs in the days before Mrs Beaton. Some useful spices – far from all of them – are aniseed, caraway, cardamom, fresh chillies, cinnamon, coriander, cumin, dill seed, fennel, fenugreek, ginger root, paprika and sesame seeds.

CHAPTER I
Crudités

There is no finer way of serving fresh young vegetables than raw, either plain or marinated in one or a combination of sauces. Spend time deciding how best to slice, arrange and present them, so that flavours, colours and textures complement or, if necessary, contradict each other. This chapter includes only a selection of ways to prepare and marinate raw vegetables; others will be found in following chapters.

CARROTS

Grate 3 carrots finely, put them into a bowl and toss them with a dressing of 2 teaspoons of lemon juice, 2 tablespoons of olive oil, seasoning and a pinch of sugar. Leave for 3 hours. They will soak up all the dressing.

CAULIFLOWER

The simplest and best way is to break the cauliflower into florets and to serve it as it is, dipping the pieces in sea salt as you eat them.

CHICORY

If you cut chicory, be sure to use a stainless steel knife, because carbon steel ones have a chemical reaction on the plant, making it bitter. You can either tear the leaves from the base, wash them and serve them as they are, or trim off the base, cut the vegetable into round segments and serve it with the following sauce. Hard-boil an egg, pound the yolk with ½ teaspoon of mustard, salt and pepper; then add a little wine vinegar and lastly 1½ tablespoons of olive oil. Toss the chicory in this dressing until every scrap is covered; the dressing should be thick and this amount will be enough for 2 or 3 chicory plants.

FLORENTINE FENNEL

Cut the hearts from the fennel and sprinkle them with lemon juice to stop them turning brown. Serve the vegetable like this or grate the bulb and let it marinate in a *vinaigrette* with crushed fennel seeds added to sharpen the flavour.

FRESH HERBS

A bowl of chopped fresh herbs is excellent served with warm bread. I prefer parsley as it comes, in sprigs, but it can be chopped and mixed in a bowl with chives, mint and cress. If you grow tarragon, fennel, borage or burnet, use and enjoy them in this way. Both sweet basil and bush basil are superb in tomato salad, and I for one would happily eat this fragrant herb plain.

LEEKS

Cut them in half lengthways to make cleaning simple. Extract the white and lime-green centres, cut them across into 2-inch lengths and then downwards into millimetre strands. Toss them well in *sauce vinaigrette*.

ONIONS

Peel them, then slice them finely in circles – so finely that the circles are almost transparent. Chop some fresh parsley and mix it with the onions. Season, then pour over wine vinegar and leave for a few hours. Before serving, drain the vinegar from the onions and keep it to use again. This method softens the onions a little and also modifies their pungency.

PARSNIPS

A vegetable mistakenly despised by some. Peel 3 parsnips, then grate them and toss in a dressing made from a pinch of curry powder, a teaspoon of honey, a teaspoon of wine vinegar and 1½ tablespoons of olive oil, plus salt and pepper. Like carrots, they will soak up a tremendous amount of dressing.

PEPPERS

As a matter of aesthetics, choose small peppers, both red and green, and cut them finely in circles. Serve them without a dressing or cut them lengthways in as frail strips as possible and soak them in a *sauce vinaigrette*.

RADISHES

Our native English radish is so good that it needs nothing but washing and trimming. The round Californian variety that we import in winter is so insipid that it is best grated and mixed with a dressing which includes either chilli or tabasco sauce. The long Mediterranean radish should be cut lengthways into slim pencil shapes, to be dipped in salt as you eat it.

RED CABBAGE

This is particularly good when grated and left to marinate in a dressing. The central stem of this, and other types of cabbages and of cauliflowers, generally thrown away, can also be grated and marinated. In Welsh mining villages in the Depression, this part of the cabbage was thought of as a delicacy and was given to children as a special treat.

SPRING ONIONS AND WATERCRESS

These need nothing but trimming, washing and arranging.

CHAPTER II

Dressings and Sauces

Sauces for Raw Vegetables

MAYONNAISE

Use 2 egg yolks, ½ teaspoon of wine vinegar or lemon juice, salt, pepper and ¼ pint (150 ml) olive oil (2 yolks will absorb more oil if you wish to make more mayonnaise).

Take the eggs out of the refrigerator some time in advance – eggs, oil and bowl or blender should all be at room temperature. Mix together the yolks, vinegar and seasoning. (If making the garlic mayonnaise, *aïoli*, it is at this stage that you add the juice crushed from 2 or more cloves of garlic.) Then start adding the oil, drop by drop, blending each drop in before you add the next; this process is best controlled if you pour the oil from a small jug. Go very slowly to start with, but as the mixture begins to emulsify and to become creamy, speed up until you are adding the oil in a thin stream as you mix. When all the oil is incorporated, you can adjust the flavour by adding a little more seasoning or vinegar.

In Mediterranean countries I have used a bowl and a wooden spoon. It takes some time, but it is highly satisfying to see the mayonnaise become thick and creamy. In London I use a blender. Both methods produce the occasional failure, but this is due to my impatient nature – I have added the oil too quickly to start with.

PISTACHIO MAYONNAISE

Grind ¼ lb (100 g) of pistachio nuts in the blender, then proceed as for a plain mayonnaise by adding the wine vinegar, egg yolks, oil and seasoning to the powdered nuts. Finish the sauce by adding a handful of finely chopped basil or parsley.

SAUCE RÉMOULADE

I have never known this to curdle and prefer it to ordinary mayonnaise with *crudités* because it is slightly less rich though just as creamy.

Hard-boil 2 eggs and mix their yolks with the yolk of 1 raw egg, either by pounding them in a bowl or by mixing them in a blender. Add seasoning, a teaspoon of lemon juice and a teaspoon of freshly chopped chives, basil or tarragon. Then slowly pour in ¼ pint (150 ml) of olive oil, mixing all the time. It will take more oil; it depends on the quantity you need. The original recipe requires a teaspoon of mustard, but I prefer it without.

SAUCE VERTE

Take 5 or 6 washed spinach leaves, strip them from their stalks, then poach them very gently in a little butter until soft. Add to this half a bunch of watercress and a good handful of parsley sprigs, again ensuring that there are no stalks on either. Stir over a low flame with a wooden spoon for about 1 minute, so that these are just softened too, then leave them to cool and let the liquid drain off (this may be kept for soup). Pound all in a bowl and extract any fibres that appear. I fear you cannot use the blender for this, because spinach has so much water that the resulting *purée* will be too wet. Hence, it must be pounded by hand. It may still be too damp. If so, place it back in a pan over a tiny heat and stir until it is a dry compact *purée*. The true and classic manner with *sauce verte* is now to add this to a mayonnaise, but there is always a chance that they won't combine, or that the mayonnaise suddenly in contact with the strong mineral content of the vegetables may curdle with shock. Therefore I combine the green *purée* with *sauce rémoulade*. It makes a ⌐stiff sauce, light green in colour. If you are lucky enough to grow sorrel, then sometimes use that instead of the spinach, parsley and watercress. A wholly different sauce results – one that tastes vaguely, yet deliciously, of gooseberries.

SAUCE POIREAUX (LEEK PURÉE)

This sauce is similar to the above, but with a flavouring *purée* of leeks. Many recipes for preparing and cooking leeks are wasteful of time and of food value – the French tradition is to use only the white part and to throw away the green leaves. This is not necessary for most leek dishes, but one should be careful in this sauce to extract the more fibrous parts of the leek and to keep them for soup.

Take ½ lb (225 g) of leeks, cut off the roots, then slice the tops into a pyramid shape, which will cut most of the green fibrous leaves away and keep the paler green stem in the centre. Tear off any other fibrous matter with your hands, then cut the leek in half lengthways. This makes washing so much easier, because you can then plainly see where the mud is. Slice the leeks across into ¼-inch strips or less. Cook them gently in a little olive oil for about 3 minutes (depending on the toughness of the leeks – old ones may need a little more); leave them to cool and drain off all the liquid for soup. Place the leeks in a blender and liquidize. More moisture will then appear, so strain again. Ensure that it is as dry as possible by squeezing it in the hands. Add it to the *rémoulade* – or use in other ways, which will appear in subsequent recipes.

SAUCE TARTARE

I consider it is best made with a *rémoulade*, rather than with the plain mayonnaise. To the *rémoulade* add the zest from the peel of 2 lemons, 2 finely chopped gherkins and a tablespoon each of capers and chopped fresh tarragon.

WALNUT AND CHESTNUT SAUCE

¼ lb (100 g) dried chestnuts
¼ lb (100 g) chopped walnuts
2 cloves garlic
juice of 2 lemons
1 cup (300 ml) olive oil
salt and pepper

Pour boiling water over the chestnuts to cover them well and leave them to soak for 1 hour. Boil them then in the soaking liquid for an hour, but check frequently that they have not used up all the liquid – they will need quite strong simmering. When they are soft and break easily with the point of a knife, take them from the heat and leave them to cool.

Crush the garlic and put it in the blender with the lemon juice, then turn on the machine until the garlic becomes well blended and the lemon juice creamy. Drain the water off the chestnuts and blend them into the garlic–lemon mixture. The *purée* will be extremely thick and the machine may not even turn, so add the olive oil to the chestnuts until the mixture acquires the texture of a good mayonnaise. Turn out into a bowl, season and mix in the chopped walnuts. This sauce is splendid with celery, endive and white cabbage.

SAUCE MOUTARDE

2 tbsp *Meaux* mustard
3 tbsp boiling water
¼ pt (150 ml) olive oil
juice and zest of 1 lemon
1 tbsp chopped parsley or tarragon
salt and pepper

Measure the mustard out into a mixing bowl, then add the boiling water slowly, stirring and beating with a wooden spoon. When the water has been absorbed, start pouring in the olive oil slowly, beating all the time. Finally, add the lemon juice and zest, herbs and seasoning.

MUSTARD AND EGG SAUCE

Elizabeth David quotes a pre-1914 English recipe for an English Salad Sauce.* As a nation, we obviously disdained real mayonnaise, and this is a combination of the basic *rémoulade*, but with cream instead of olive oil. Because of the excellence of *Meaux* mustard, I have changed the recipe, thus making it easier to create.

Pound 2 cooked egg yolks with a teaspoon of mustard. Add 1 raw egg yolk and and little seasoning; then stir in ¼ pint (150 ml) of thick cream. It is a lovely shade of rich yellow,

* In *Spices, Salt and Aromatics in the English Kitchen*, Elizabeth David, Penguin Books.

slightly speckled from the mustard seed. Sticks of celery seem to gravitate towards this sauce.

Variation: Watercress and Egg Sauce
The same recipe as above, but with the mustard omitted and watercress and lemon juice added.

Chop the leaves of a bunch of watercress finely and mix it with the egg yolks and seasoning. Pour in the juice of a lemon and mix together thoroughly again before adding the cream.

SAUCE À LA CRÈME

Melt 3 oz (75 g) of butter in a thick-bottomed saucepan, season with salt, pepper and a little nutmeg, then add ¼ pt (150 ml) of double cream. Take away from the heat and stir vigorously.

TOMATO SAUCE

There is no point in using tomatoes from English shops or markets; their flavour is nil. So attempt to make this sauce only if you have home-grown tomatoes.

Skin 1 lb (450 g): pour boiling water over them and leave them for a minute – the skin will then peel away easily. Chop the flesh and discard any hard centre. Place the tomatoes in a saucepan with a tablespoon of olive oil, 3 crushed cloves of garlic, a sliced shallot and a teaspoon of dried marjoram. If you have fresh basil, omit the marjoram and add chopped basil after the sauce has been cooked. If you have no shallot use an onion. Season the mixture and allow the tomatoes to simmer gently for about a quarter of an hour. Allow to cool, then liquidize into a thick pulp. Check the seasoning; it all depends upon the tomatoes. Sometimes they might need a squeeze of lemon juice, at other times, a small glass of red wine won't do any harm, added as they cook. The resulting sauce should be a thick enough *purée* to coat the back of a spoon. Reheat it before serving – the hot sauce is excellent with the cold *crudités*. It can be made from tinned tomatoes, but the flavour is quite different and, in my opinion, not worth the trouble.

CURRY SAUCE*

Home-made curry powder will be better than any commercial brand. You can vary the flavour and regulate the heat – which depends on the use of dried chillies – to your taste. The following combination of spices makes an aromatic powder which is not hot.

Take a generous tablespoonful each of cardamom pods, sesame, cumin, coriander, cloves, black peppercorns, allspice and aniseed. Extract the black seeds from the cardamom pods, mix them with the rest of the spices, spread them on a baking sheet and cook them in a medium-hot oven for half an hour. Cool them, then grind them as powdery as possible with a mortar and pestle, which is hard work, or in a coffee grinder or an electric blender, which is no work at all.

This powder will keep for many months in an airtight jar, ready for use, and can be enhanced for particular dishes by adding ground nutmeg, mace, mustard and poppy seeds, fenugreek, cinnamon or ginger. The characteristic colour of curry comes from turmeric, but this quickly loses its flavour and aroma, so cannot be relied on to add much to the taste. To release the flavour of the curry powder, *sauté* it in oil or butter (the Indians use a clarified butter called ghee).

Now for the sauce to use with *crudités*.

1 tbsp curry powder
1 grated ginger root
3 crushed cloves of garlic
vegetable oil
½ lb (225 g) lentils cooked to a thick *purée*

Stir the curry powder, ginger and garlic into a little vegetable oil for a few minutes over a gentle heat, then add the *purée* of lentils and go on stirring till it is heated through. If you want to make this sauce fiery, add *Chilli Sauce* (see page 34). Two teaspoonfuls of this will make it very hot.

* Another recipe for curry powder from *Indian Domestic Economy* (1850) is quoted by Elizabeth David in *Spices, Salt and Aromatics in the English Kitchen*.

CUCUMBER AND YOGHURT SAUCE (JAJIKI)

This is eaten all over the Middle East and in Greece, and is particularly cool and refreshing, especially if the *Curry Sauce* is also upon the table.

Do not peel the cucumber. Slice it lengthways into 8 strips, then cut it across into ¼-inch pieces. Place it in a colander and sprinkle with salt. Leave it for 2 hours so that it loses much of its water, then wash the salt from it beneath a tap. Chop a handful of fresh mint; if there is none, use parsley or basil, though mint is the most usual and refreshing. Grind a little pepper over the cucumber and add it and the fresh herb to as much yoghurt as will make a liquid but chunky sauce.

SALSA AGRODOLCE (SWEET-AND-SOUR SAUCE)

1 large sliced onion
1 grated carrot
olive oil
1 tbsp malt vinegar
1 tbsp soy sauce
1 tbsp each sultanas and broken almonds
1 tsp crushed cloves
2 tbsp honey
1 tbsp grated bitter chocolate

Gently cook the onion and carrot in some olive oil for about 3 minutes or until the onion is soft. Pour in the vinegar and soy sauce, then add the sultanas, almonds, cloves and honey. Stir well and keep the sauce simmering. At the last minute, add the chocolate, which will give a little body to the sauce. Taste and check the seasoning. At this stage, one quite often has to add either a little more vinegar or honey to ensure that the sweetness and the sourness are well balanced.

GREEN SAUCE

¼ pt (150 ml) olive oil
2 tsp wine vinegar
6 oz (175 g) capers
3 crushed cloves of garlic
handful of chopped parsley
salt and pepper

In a bowl, mix all the ingredients well together. The sauce
should be thick and chunky.

GREEN SAUCE WITH HORSERADISH

¼ pt (150 ml) olive oil
2 tbsp grated fresh horseradish
2 tbsp breadcrumbs
handful of chopped parsley
salt and pepper

Mix together all the ingredients in a bowl. If it is too thick,
add a little wine vinegar.

SAUCE MESSINE

½ pt (300 ml) single cream
3 oz (75 g) butter
1 tsp flour
3 chopped spring onions
1 tsp finely chopped parsley, chervil and tarragon
zest from 1 lemon
2 egg yolks
salt and pepper

Make a *roux* with the butter and flour. It will be very thin, so
the flour will cook quickly. Put into the pan the spring onions,
herbs, mustard and lemon zest and stir for another minute.
Take it from the heat and pour in the cream; heat again until
the sauce begins to thicken, remove from the heat again and
add the egg yolks. Bring the sauce back slowly to its former
heat, but without boiling. You want the yolks to thicken the
sauce, not to turn them into scrambled eggs. Season.

The next two sauces are not for use with crudités, *but they are
needed so often in cooking that I must include them.*

WHITE SAUCE OR SAUCE BÉCHAMEL

½ pt (300 ml) milk
3 bay leaves
salt and pepper
1 oz (25 g) butter
1 oz (25 g) flour

Heat the milk with the bay leaves and the seasoning. Melt the butter in a thick-bottomed pan, add the flour and stir over a low heat for a couple of minutes. It mustn't brown, but it should froth and bubble a little; this ensures the flour is cooked. Remove the pan from the heat, take the bay leaves out of the milk and add the milk, bit by bit, to the *roux*. Stir the mixture vigorously with a wooden spoon to blend it smoothly between each addition. Put it back on the heat and let it cook gently, stirring all the time, for a few minutes, until it has thickened and is quite smooth. In my experience, this amount of flour to milk makes a thin to medium sauce, though the authors of *Mastering the Art of French Cooking** claim it makes a thick sauce.

CHEESE SAUCE OR SAUCE MORNAY

Add 4 oz (100 g) of grated cheese to a *White Sauce* after stirring the milk into the *roux*, and go on stirring until it has all melted. The kind of cheese used depends on the type of sauce required. A light sauce could be made with Gruyère and a little Parmesan, and a stronger one from an English cheese such as Double Gloucester or Sage Derby (or, for that matter, from a good flavoury mousetrap cheese).

My last three sauces are ones that I use more than any others – but there is a snag about the first two. They both require fresh basil, so can be made only in summer or autumn by those who have managed to grow it. I have the luck to spend a lot of time in the Mediterranean, where it is no problem. In England, your pot of basil will need a sheltered sunny corner – and a good summer: or it can be successfully grown from seed inside if placed in the sunniest room.

* *Mastering the Art of French Cooking*, Simone Beck, Louiseet Bertholle, Julia Child, Penguin Books.

AÏLLADE

1 head of garlic
6 fresh tomatoes
handful of chopped basil
salt and pepper
¼ pt (150 ml) olive oil

Peel the garlic (easily done if you first pour boiling water over the cloves as you do with tomatoes). Chop the tomatoes coarsely, doing it over the bowl of the blender to avoid losing any juices. Liquidize them with the garlic, basil and seasoning, then add the olive oil. Blend to the consistency of thick soup. The sauce is then ready to be used in cooking, or can be eaten with pasta or *crudités*.

PESTO

This sauce is sometimes confused with *Aïllade*, a confusion existing because the individual cook may – and often does – add garlic to it. People who think that *Aïllade* and *Pesto* are the same thing, sometimes call this one *Pistou*, but that is just the French name for *Pesto*. The difference is that in my *Pesto/Pistou* I use pistachio nuts and no garlic (in Genoa, they use pine nuts); nor do I care much for the addition of hard cheese.

handful of chopped basil
¼ lb (100 g) pistachio nuts
6 tomatoes
¾ pt (400 ml) olive oil
salt and pepper

Blend everything together, as for an *Aïllade*. The resulting mixture will be made somewhat thicker by the pistachio nuts.

GARLIC CREAM

This by-product of *Garlic Soup* (see page 51) is my own invention and has never yet let a dish down. The flavour it imparts is both subtle and highly distinctive; because the garlic has been so thoroughly cooked, it is not always recognized. The cream has many uses, as will be seen in the recipes in this book.

Make the soup, but do not add the egg yolks. Pour it into a screw-top bottle and store it in the refrigerator. After a few hours, it will separate, the oil carrying the garlic *purée* to the top of the bottle like a thick cream. Skim this off with a spoon as you need it, or bottle it separately. The clear liquid left in the bottle can be used in a *White Vegetable Stock* (see page 45).

CHAPTER III

Vegetable Purées

Dried Beans and Peas

The pulses – all kinds of beans and peas – are the seeds of
leguminous plants, so-called because they contain a protein
substance, legumin, named by the analyst who discovered it
early in the nineteenth century. It is akin to casein, the main
protein in milk and the substance which, when coagulated
with acid, forms the basis of cheese.

The pulses contain two or three times the amount of protein
of cereals. They are still cheap, go a long way, and are
satisfying and delicious when prepared with herbs and spices.
However, they have one drawback. As Sir Thomas Blount
remarked dourly in the seventeenth century, 'Peas and beans
are flatulent meat'. Cookery books tend to be prudish and
avoid mentioning this fact, but the reliable Elizabeth David
quotes a recipe* for *cassoulet* from Auguste Columbié in the
latter half of the nineteenth century which includes his remedy.
He advises bringing beans to the boil after soaking them, then
removing them from the fire and leaving them for 40 minutes.
Their liquid should be siphoned into bottles, well corked and
kept for removing obstinate stains from linen. He warns that
the liquid must never be washed down the sink, because the
stench will linger in the kitchen for days. I have followed his
directions faithfully; there was no stench. Nor, alas, did the
beans become any less flatulent. The white haricot beans
grown in the districts of Soissons and Arpajon in the last
century must have contained so much oxide of potassium that
they were positively poisonous.

However, using my friends and myself as guinea pigs, I
have done some experimenting with quite useful results.

* Elizabeth David, *French Provincial Cooking*, Penguin Handbooks.

First, I am now certain that leaving pulses to soak in one lot of water for 24 hours makes matters worse; having released their oxide of potassium into the water, they then soak it up again. A fresh pulse of good quality (bought from a reliable shop with a high turnover) swells to three times its size within an hour, if boiling water is poured over it. So I pour off the water within the hour – indeed, I pour off the first water after 5 minutes and repeat the process three times. The 'gas' is thus poured away before it can be reabsorbed, and the constant onslaught by scalding water helps to break down the beans' structure and therefore to lessen the cooking time.

I am indebted to Rosemary Hemphill's *Herbs for All Seasons** for another and even better antidote. She points out that aniseed, fennel and caraway are old German remedies for flatulence, and that a tea made from them will eliminate the discomfort. I have found that cooking pulses with one of these or crushing the seeds and mixing them into the *purée* does indeed appear to diminish the pulse's disquieting effect.

Continental delicatessens, Health Food and Cypriot shops have the widest variety of pulses. The preparation is the same for all, but the cooking time varies from a few minutes to several hours. Lentils will triple in bulk when soaked within a quarter of an hour and can cook inside 5 minutes, while red kidney beans can take up to 5 hours in a slow oven. It is the nature of pulses to soak up the flavour of whatever herbs, spices, oils or vegetables you wish them to reflect, whether bland or spicy. They also lend themselves to a great number of variations.

The following are basic bean recipes which any cook can pursue further. You can add to them minced onion, grated raw carrot and any kind of fresh herb you like. *Tahina* can also be combined with them, as can ground almonds or chopped nuts of various kinds. A lighter, less earthy quality can be obtained by mixing a bean *purée* with mayonnaise – a superb fusion of peasant cooking and the great French tradition.

Whatever else you may add, three ingredients are vital. Lemon juice 'lifts' the earthy pulses and seems to aerate their heaviness, olive oil gives them creaminess, and – to me at any rate – garlic is essential to the character of pulse dishes.

* Rosemary Hemphill, *Herbs for All Seasons*, Angus & Robertson.

Though using a blender helps to make all these *purées* – especially the aubergine ones – quickly, most of them can be made in a bowl by mashing the ingredients together with a wooden spoon.

BROAD BEAN PURÉE

These are the dried beans that are broken, thus making the cooking time far less than if they were left whole. The Greeks eat them as a salad, sprinkled with fresh herbs and olive oil.

¼ lb (100 g) dried broad beans
5 bay leaves
1 lemon
2 crushed cloves of garlic
1 tbsp aniseed
handful of chopped parsley or mint
1 tbsp olive oil
salt and pepper

After throwing away the water that the beans have been soaking in for the third time (see chapter introduction), add 1 pint (600 ml) of cold water to them, with the bay leaves and the zest of the lemon. Simmer gently for 45 minutes; in that time the beans should soak up all the liquid and disintegrate into a mush. Allow them to cool and throw away the bay leaves. The beans will have taken on the flavour of the bay and the lemon zest – the smell while they are cooking is fragrant. Place them in a bowl, add the garlic, the juice of the lemon and the aniseed and fresh herbs. Stir in the olive oil and work the mixture into a paste. Season, cover and keep in the refrigerator. Eat with warm Greek bread as a *mezze* before a meal or with other *purées* as a first course.

HARICOT BEAN PURÉE WITH CARAWAY

These dried beans, if fresh, seem to break up beneath the scalding very easily, but they are hungry for water, so ensure that plenty is used for the cooking. It is easier to judge how much seasoning a dish needs when the beans are blended with the other flavourings, so add it at that stage. After soaking in the usual way (see chapter introduction), the beans will need about an hour and a half to cook; by then they will have used up much of the liquid. Drain the beans and reserve the liquid for soup, if you need it. Grind a tablespoon of caraway seeds in the mortar. Allow the beans to cool.

To make the *purée*, use an electric blender if you have one, as the resulting cream is smoother. Liquidize the cooled beans with the juice of 2 lemons, 2 crushed cloves of garlic, the caraway and seasoning. The *purée* should be thick enough to stop the blades turning, so pour in 2 tablespoons of olive oil. Within a minute the mixture will become as smooth as thick cream and a light oatmeal colour. The caraway, nutty and slightly peppermint in flavour, gives the modest bean a subtle aromatic piquancy which is a far cry from the seed-cake of childhood.

PURÉE OF GREEN PEAS AND CHILLI SAUCE

    10 green or red chillies
    ¼ lb (100 g) dried green peas
    juice of 1 lemon
    1 tbsp aniseed
    salt and pepper
    3 tbsp olive oil

Chop the chillies, after cutting off their stalks, and put them in a blender with ½ pint (300 ml) of water. Reduce them to a pulp. This is a basic hot sauce, which can be put in a screw-top bottle and kept in the refrigerator for use when you need it. For this dish, however, the peas, after their soaking, are cooked in the chilli water. This rather obstinate and faceted dried pulse will need 3 hours cooking (see chapter introduction). They must be checked every 40 minutes to ensure that they have not cooked themselves dry, so it is best to be generous with the water. They are cooked when they begin to disintegrate, and will by then have taken on the fiery flavour of the chillies.

Place the peas in the blender with the lemon juice, aniseed, seasoning, not more than 2 tablespoons of the water they cooked in and the olive oil. Blend to a smooth *purée*. It might need a drop more water, but make certain first that all the oil has become amalgamated.

These are the dullest of all the pulses, but cooking them with the chillies gives them a subliminal kick; the spiced fire of their flavour is noticeable only after each mouthful. It is, though, a dish only for those who are addicted to curries or to *chilli con carne*.

RED CHINESE BEAN PURÉE

From Chinese stores one can buy red, black or yellow beans, small and round, with spots. The red beans, when cooked, end up the colour of borsch – dark ruby, tinged with purple. Soak 6 ozs (175 g) of beans for an hour (renew the water 3 times) and they will cook within an hour. This *purée* uses 2 oz (50 g) of grated ginger root, which is stirred into a little hot oil to release its flavour Do this in the pan you will use for the beans. Add the soaked beans and enough water to allow them to double their bulk. It is another slightly fiery *purée*, but I believe that these beans need this type of assistance to make them really interesting.

Let us now look at two pulses which do not provoke flatulence – or certainly not to the same degree: chick peas and lentils. The first, which I consider the Emperor of Pulses, makes the hummus *always served in Greek and Turkish restaurants. If you found it a little dull when you ate it in a restaurant, that will have been the restaurant's fault; well made, it is delicious.*

HUMMUS

Prepare 6 oz (175 g) chick peas by pouring boiling water over them and leaving them to soak and swell for an hour. They will then need a good hour and a half's cooking. This pulse will not disintegrate into a mush, but is done when the point of a knife enters one easily and it breaks apart.

Put the cooked peas in the blender with a tablespoon of lemon juice and 4 crushed cloves of garlic, and ¼ pint (150 ml) of olive oil. If the resultant *purée* is so thick that the blender refuses to work, add a little of the water in which you cooked the chick peas. And if you make it too thin by mistake, do not worry. The charm of making *hummus* is that you can remedy such a mistake with ease by adding, for example, cottage cheese, grated Parmesan, the pounded yolks of hard-boiled eggs or ground almonds. Each of these will, of course, produce a variation on the original theme, but it will be good.

The traditional dish uses no such extras, only fresh mint – it is the mint which is often omitted by restaurant cooks, which is a pity. *Hummus* is already much lighter than the other bean or pea *purées*, and the mint and lemon juice stress this fineness. Emphasize it further by mixing it fiercely and long, and if you want it to be even airier, fold in the stiffly whipped white of an egg or two. This produces a dish as light as a *soufflé* but with the peasant character of its origins.

The adaptability of *hummus* is remarkable and is worthy of much exploring. It can be used in soups, or bound with an egg, shaped into *falafel* (little cakes) and fried. Also, it can be mixed with other ingredients and used as a filling in *crêpes*.

LENTIL PURÉE

All recipes I know say lentils should be soaked and cooked for up to an hour. This is not true. Lentils plunged into boiling water will cook in 8 to 10 minutes without any previous soaking, and that is sufficient time if they are to be eaten as a salad. (For *Lentil Soup* see page 47). After 10 minutes they will soften and disintegrate, and you will lose much of their food value in the water. This does not matter if the liquid is kept for soup, but most of us cannot hoard vegetable stock for soup unless we have a large and hungry family.

Drain 8 oz (225 g) of cooked lentils and put them in a blender with a tablespoon of lemon juice and 2 crushed cloves of garlic. Add 3 tablespoons of olive oil, as for the other pulse *purées*, and any fresh herbs you choose. The mixture will become very liquid and seem more like soup, so add enough breadcrumbs (about 2–3 oz, or 50–75 g) to stiffen it into a paste. The golden colour of this *purée* is a great attraction.

Like *hummus*, it can also be bound with an egg and fried as *falafel* – a splendid hot appetizer.

The following purées *are sometimes referred to as* pâtés; *the nomenclature is up to the whim of the cook or restaurant. Sometimes their consistency tends more towards a paste than a* purée. *But 'paste' in England reminds one of those jars of tasteless, gummy potted meat – quite unlike these light and fragrant* purées. *I have tended in this book to use the French words because of their appetizing associations, and sometimes there is no English equivalent (as in* mollet, *see page* 71*). Often, in France, the recipe has been named after the dish that it is cooked in, but even here there is confusion, for* pâté *and* terrine *are used in an arbitrary fashion. One word I have avoided: the hideous American importation, 'dip'. All the* purées *in this chapter can be scooped up with warm Greek bread or spread on toast or fresh home-made bread. They can all, it is true, be dipped into with* crudités. *But 'dip', with its perky clipped sound, deadens the taste buds and is quite wrong for the subtle union of oils, spices, herbs and fresh vegetables, which these mixtures are.*

However, names should be as exact as possible, so I would suggest that when the vegetable is united with olive oil and remains light in consistency, it is a purée; *when it is united with butter or cream and kept in a refrigerator, it becomes a* pâté *or a paste.*

AVOCADO PURÉE

The time to make this is when the avocados are cheap, when on the market stalls they look black, soft and over-ripe. Stall-holders often sell them at a much reduced price then, and if you choose well, discarding the ones that have become mushy to the slightest pressure, you can acquire a bargain. Even avocados which have gone partly black inside will often yield a good deal of flesh which is still all right.

2 avocados
1 lemon
salt and pepper
2 cloves of garlic
¼ pt (150 ml) olive oil

Scrape the zest from the lemon skin, then squeeze the juice. Put both into the blender, with the salt, pepper and garlic. Mix well. Now add all the flesh from the avocados and blend again into a pulp. As if it were a mayonnaise, add the olive oil slowly until the pulp has consumed all it can. The resulting mixture should be a heavy, smooth cream of the palest green, and it is so rich that a little of it goes a long way. It is not only fairly cheap, but also deliciously exotic.

A variation on this creates a superb iced soup (see page 65), and a mixture of equal amounts of this *purée* and mayonnaise makes yet another sauce that goes well with *crudités*. It can also be used for stuffed eggs: pound the hard-boiled yolks with the *purée* and pile the mixture into the cavity of the whites.

PURÉE DE FÈVES

In February, we begin to import broad beans from Cyprus and Crete. They seem expensive, but when you consider that the pods can be used as well as the beans, I feel they are good value. You can use pods alone for this delicious *purée*, if you wish, provided they are young and tender. For a stronger flavour, use the whole vegetable – pod and bean.

Choose 1 lb (450 g) of young broad beans; they should be tender enough to eat raw. Top and tail them, break the pods into pieces and simmer for 5 minutes in a little salted water. Drain off the liquid, which can be used for soup. Place the pods in a blender, add a little of the liquid they have cooked in, a hefty grind of black pepper, 1 oz (25 g) of butter and 2 tablespoons of cream. Blend to a thick pulp. Sieve. It is best eaten slightly warm. Peas may also be used in this way, and they too must be caught when they are young. A most satisfactory *purée* can be made from *mange-tout* as well.

PURÉE OF SPINACH

If you adore spinach as I do, then a bowl of this with perhaps *purées* of the avocado and of two pulses makes a blissful start to a meal. The only trouble with spinach is its high water content. As it gives the water up in cooking (don't add any), it shrinks in volume, so you must start with a large saucepan-full to end with quite a small bowl of *purée*.

After carefully washing the leaves, cook 1 lb (450 g) of spinach without water, but with a tiny amount of butter. Stir with a wooden spoon to stop it sticking; it will be cooked in 5 minutes or less.

Cool the spinach a bit, then squeeze it dry with the hands and chop it up finely. Don't use a blender for the chopping, because the spinach will only generate more liquid which will have to be drained. Over a gentle heat melt 2 oz (50 g) of butter. Work the chopped spinach into the melted butter with a wooden spoon – one is in fact almost crushing it, and the spinach will soak up the butter *ad infinitum*. Pour it into a bowl and after a moment, when it has cooled a little, add a tablespoon of thick cream; season and mix well. It is best served when slightly warm. If kept in the refrigerator, the butter will make it hard and like a paste (or *pâté*) – quite pleasant, but with a less good flavour than that achieved at a warmer temperature. Some people enjoy grated nutmeg with spinach, and you can cook a chopped clove of garlic in the butter before adding the spinach.

PURÉE OF OLIVES

I prefer the flavour of black olives, but one can make this from green ones just as well. Take 4 oz (100 g) of olives. Stone them and then place them in the blender with a tablespoon of lemon juice, 2 crushed cloves of garlic and a pinch of black pepper. Add 3 tablespoons of olive oil slowly, as you would for mayonnaise. This will need no salt, because the olives will be salty from their brine, but a teaspoon of crushed coriander goes well with black olives. As it seems too much of a contradiction for the green, I would tend to use chopped parsley or mint with them.

MUSHROOM PURÉE

If you use field mushrooms, which have a much stronger and better flavour than the cultivated ones, then the *purée* will be as black as burnt oak and will taste sensational. The preparation and cooking are the same for both kinds. Never peel the outer skin from mushrooms, for much of the flavour lies in it. Merely wash ½ lb (225 g) of them carefully and, for this recipe, discard the stalks, which are often too fibrous. Slice the mushroom caps quite thinly or, if they are field ones, just break them up with your fingers. Use 2 oz (50 g) of butter and let them cook slowly in it in a covered pan until they are soft; add seasoning and let them cool. Place the mushrooms in a blender and liquidize to a pulp, after draining the liquid away that they have made when cooking. Add to the pulp a carton of sour cream.

There is a Greek dish that cooks the mushrooms in olive oil with bay leaves and crushed coriander (see page 111). If this method is chosen, make sure you use butter instead of oil and throw away the bay leaves. The resulting *purée* adds another dimension to the mushrooms.

ARTICHOKE PÂTÉ

This *pâté* uses the rather brown and old artichokes which you can find being sold cheaply in the market, as people suspect that they are too tough or dried up inside. They are not, and 2 large ones will make enough for about five people.

2 large artichokes
1 tbsp olive oil
1 dsp wine vinegar
salt and pepper

Cut the stalks from the artichokes and boil both together in salted water for about 45 minutes. Leave them to cool, keeping the water and the stalks.

Take the leaves off the artichokes one by one and, with a sharp knife, scrape the edible part of the leaf into a bowl. This may sound a long and arduous task, but it can be done quickly and easily. Scrape away the choke and dice the delicious pad of flesh at the base. Either put all this flesh into a bowl and mash it with the other ingredients, or put it into a blender, which will give you a smooth *purée* without effort. The oil will stiffen it into a paste once it is in the refrigerator. I put the leaves with the stalks back into the water used for cooking the artichokes and boil it for another half hour for a soup or a stock.

PIPÉRADE PURÉE

For the *pipérade* recipe, see page 181. After adding the scrambled eggs to the peppers, onions, garlic and tomatoes, allow the mixture to cool, then blend it to a *purée*. This is very rich, for it is an amalgamation of all the flavours, heightened by the olive oil and the eggs.

RATATOUILLE PURÉE

Follow the recipe for *ratatouille* on page 180. Allow it to cool, then blend it to a *purée*. Though this is without eggs, it is almost as rich as the *pipérade*. Both recipes are excellent ways of reviving left-overs.

CAULIFLOWER PURÉE

1 large cauliflower
2 chopped onions
5 crushed cloves of garlic
1 piece ginger root
1 tsp turmeric powder
2 tsp mixed coriander seeds, cumin and paprika
olive oil
2 tbsp yoghurt
salt and pepper

Slice the cauliflower into small pieces and boil them in a little water with the onions. Grind the garlic, ginger root and spices into a paste and fry them gently in olive oil. Mix all the ingredients in a blender with the yoghurt until smooth.

TURNIP PURÉE

1 lb (450 g) turnips
2 chopped onions
1 grated ginger root
2 tsp aniseed
1 tsp mixed curry spices (see page 25)
1 tsp paprika
salt and pepper
oil or butter
1 carton sour cream

Peel the turnips, then slice them and boil in a little water until soft – they cook quickly. Gently fry the onions with the ginger root, spices and seasoning in the oil or butter. Drain the turnips with care and mix them with the onions and spices in a blender, adding the sour cream.

CARROT AND RADISH PURÉE

½ lb (225 g) carrots
½ lb (225 g) Mediterranean radishes
2 onions
1 piece ginger root
½ tsp curry powder (see page 25)
olive oil
salt and pepper

Slice the carrots, radishes and onions, and boil them in a little water until they are soft. Drain them and keep the water for stock. Grate the ginger root and cook it with the spices in a tablespoon of olive oil. Let them cook, then combine them with the vegetables and seasoning in a blender, adding more oil to achieve a smooth consistency.

AUBERGINE PURÉES

Aubergines make the most beautiful *purées*, and by adding other vegetables, different herbs and spices, and eggs and oil, one can create many variations. Some of these *purées* can be used as part of the fillings in *lasagne* and *canneloni* dishes.

1 **Melitzána**
   This is the Greek name for this dish, yet it is known all over the Middle East as well. In these countries, the split aubergines would be cooked over charcoal.
   Oil the skin of a large aubergine, put it in a preheated oven at a medium heat and leave it for an hour. The flesh inside should then be soft and cooked through. Leave it to cool, then scoop out the interior and discard the skin. Liquidize the pulp in a blender with 2 crushed cloves of garlic and the juice of a lemon. Add seasoning and pour in enough olive oil to make a thick cream.

2 **Sesame Aubergines**
   Bake 4 oz (100 g) of sesame seeds in the oven until they are golden. Add these to the cooked pulp of 2 medium aubergines, reserving a few to sprinkle over the top when the dish is served. Blend seasoning and a carton of sour cream into the vegetable until it is smooth.

3 **Aubergine, Mushroom and Olive Purée**
Sauté ¼ lb (100 g) of mushrooms in a little butter until they are soft. Stone a dozen black olives and place the mushrooms, with their liquid, the olives, 2 crushed cloves of garlic and seasoning in the blender with the cooked pulp from 2 medium aubergines. Pour in 2 tablespoons of olive oil and reduce the mixture to a *purée*. The aubergine flavour should predominate.

4 **Indian Aubergine Purée**
To the cooked pulp of 1 large aubergine, add 1 finely chopped onion, a handful of chopped coriander leaves, 1 finely chopped green chilli, a teaspoon of brown sugar, the juice of 1 lemon and salt to taste. Mix in 2 tablespoons of yoghurt and sprinkle with a little more chopped coriander leaves.

5 **Vegetable and Egg Purée**

This lies between *pipérade* and *ratatouille purées*. Slice 3 large aubergines, 4 peppers and 4 large courgettes, and *sauté* them gently in olive oil, with seasoning, for 1 hour. Add 6 beaten eggs and fold them into the mixture until the eggs are cooked. Leave to cool, then mix them in the blender until smooth.

CHAPTER IV

Soups: Hot and Iced

Hot Soups

It took me many years to discover that all manner of vegetable soups can be perfect in their own right without having a basis of meat or bone stock. A well-flavoured oil – olive, walnut or peanut – is the answer; and, for added richness, depend upon egg yolks, lemon juice, butter, cream, brandy or wine. In fact, I am quite persuaded now that vegetable soups are better without being adulterated by lard, dripping or stock made from poultry or meat bones. Some vegetarian recipes specify a meat substitute, such as Barmene or Marmite, but I have found that these spoil the flavour of the vegetables (see Preface).

It is true that a basic vegetable stock can be made from all the outside and fibrous leaves that are usually thrown away, but the stock-pot is not a dustbin. What you use should partly depend on the soup you intend to make. Too many strong flavours will merge in the stock, so that the result will be unidentifiable by the palate. It may properly be called mixed vegetable soup, but cannot be enjoyed for its particular flavour. Though salt and pepper are listed in the ingredients and instructions, it is best to be sparing with them, for they can always be adjusted at the last moment.

Knowing that so much real goodness lies in peel, some cooks make a stock from the peel of all the root vegetables (after scrubbing them well, naturally). This produces a dark nutty stock, which is a bit on the formidable side, but it can be excellent for a thick winter soup that uses dried pulses.

Many of the recipes in this book require a basic vegetable stock, in which some of the vegetables are poached. Here are the two stocks I use most often. They can be bottled and kept in the refrigerator for some weeks if necessary.

WHITE VEGETABLE STOCK

This is made from two stocks. The first is the *Garlic Soup* (see page 51). When the soup has settled for a day in the refrigerator, the garlic cream at the top is used for other dishes or bottled separately, and a clear stock is left. Mix it with the following stock.

2 coarsely chopped onions
1 coarsely chopped head of celery
3 pt (1·75 l) water
salt and pepper

Simmer the onions and the celery in the water with the seasoning for an hour. Leave to cool. Pulp the vegetables in the pan with a potato masher, stir the mixture, then pass the liquid through a fine sieve. Throw away the pulp.

BROWN VEGETABLE STOCK

2 chopped onions
1 chopped head of celery
2 tbsp olive oil
3 pt (1·75 l) boiling water
¼ pt (150 ml) soy sauce
a pinch of pepper

Sauté the vegetables in the oil over quite a fierce heat, so that they brown a little; it will take only a few minutes. Pour on the water and the soy sauce, and add the pepper. There is no need for salt with the soy sauce. Let it simmer for an hour, then mash the vegetables in the pan and pour off the liquid through a sieve. Throw away the pulp.

THICK WINTER SOUP

1 lb (450 g) sliced carrots
1 lb (450 g) sliced onions
¼ lb (100 g) dried haricot beans, soaked in 3 changes of water
for an hour
olive oil
2 crushed cloves of garlic
salt and pepper
handful of chopped celery leaves

Sauté the carrots and the onions in olive oil gently for a minute or so. Add the garlic and the seasoning, and pour the water over them. Let it all simmer for an hour.

In the meantime, cook the soaked beans in another pan, without salt. When they begin to disintegrate, take a few out with a strainer and put them to one side. Put the vegetable liquid, after it has cooled, into a blender, then add the rest of the beans and blend. Judge how thick you want the soup to be and, if necessary, add more water. Stir in the cooked vegetables and check the seasoning.

This is a hearty soup, but the beans, being bland, do not confuse the flavours of the onions and the carrots. I enjoy finding some of the beans whole, which is why I leave a few aside to add after the blending. Serve with the celery leaves sprinkled over the surface.

THICK PEA SOUP

$\frac{1}{2}$ lb (225 g) dried green peas
5 bay leaves
5 crushed cloves of garlic
2 tsp crushed caraway seeds
salt and pepper
$\frac{1}{2}$ pt (300 ml) *Brown Vegetable Stock* (see page 45)
$\frac{1}{2}$ pt (300 ml) yoghurt

Pour boiling water over the dried peas, let them soak in it; drain, and repeat the process within an hour. The peas should have swelled to three times their size.

Put them into a large casserole with 3 pints (1·75 l) boiling water, the bay leaves, garlic, caraway seeds and seasoning. Preheat the oven to 350°F/180°C/Gas Mark 4, and place the casserole on a low rack in it. Cook the peas for an hour, then lower the heat to 250°F/120°C/Gas Mark $\frac{1}{4}$, and check that they still have plenty of water. These are the most unreliable of the dried pulses, as some soak up more water than others. Add more water to keep them from drying out, if necessary. Continue cooking the peas until they are soft, let them cool, discard the bay leaves and blend to a thick *purée*.

Now reheat the *purée* with the *Brown Vegetable Stock* and, just before serving, stir in the yoghurt away from the heat.

Or, if you have a soup tureen in which to serve the soup, heat the tureen, pour in the hot soup and then stir in the yoghurt.

SPLIT PEA SOUP

¼ lb (100 g) dried split peas
2 chopped onions
2 crushed cloves of garlic
2 oz (50 g) butter
3–4 pt (1·75–2·2 l) boiling water
juice and zest from 2 lemons
salt and pepper
½ pt (300 ml) single cream
1 tbsp chopped parsley

Soak the split peas for an hour, using the three-change method (see page 32). Drain. Melt the butter in a saucepan, add the onions, garlic and peas, and cook them together for a few minutes over a low flame. Add the water and the juice and zest from the lemons. Simmer the mixture on top of the stove for an hour. Cool, then blend to a milky-white thin *purée*.

If it seems too thick, add a little of the *White Vegetable Stock* (see page 45). Taste and check the seasoning. Reheat and, just before serving, add the cream. Sprinkle the top of the soup with the parsley and serve.

LENTIL SOUP

¼ lb (100 g) lentils
2 chopped onions
2 crushed cloves of garlic
2 oz (50 g) butter
juice and zest from 2 lemons
salt and pepper
½ pt (300 ml) single cream
1 tbsp chopped parsley

Pour boiling water over the lentils. They will be ready to be cooked within 10 minutes. Make this soup as for the *Split Pea Soup* above, but simmer the lentils for only 30 minutes, if that.

PUMPKIN SOUP

This is really one of the great soups, and I have never known anyone to be content with one serving.

2 lb (1 kg) pumpkin flesh (or half a large pumpkin)
3 oz (75 g) butter
salt and pepper
1 pt (600 ml) boiling water
2 pt (1·1 l) *White Vegetable Stock* (see page 45)

Scoop out all the pumpkin flesh and throw away the seeds. Dice and *sauté* the flesh in the butter with the seasoning. It will quickly absorb the butter and begin to soften. Add the water and let the pumpkin simmer on top of the stove for 10 minutes. Then add the vegetable stock. Allow the mixture to cool, then *purée* it in a blender. This soup should be fairly thin, very smooth and golden in colour.

BROAD BEAN SOUP

Take the beans from the pods, but don't throw the pods away. Instead, boil them for 15 minutes in enough water to cover them, and allow them to cool. Blend them, then put the liquid through a fine sieve.

Sauté the beans in 2 oz (50 g) of butter, then pour 2 pints (1·1 l) of boiling water over them, and season with *gros sel* and a lot of black pepper. Cook until tender, allow to cool, then blend to a thick *purée*. Add the water from the pods and reheat the soup. At the last moment, add ¼ pt (150 ml) of single cream.

JERUSALEM ARTICHOKE SOUP

Prepare the Jerusalem artichokes according to the method on page 179. This takes all of the trouble out of this delicious but knobbly root vegetable.

Put the cooked artichokes, with their stock, into a blender and *purée* them. Transfer them to a saucepan, slowly add ½ pint (300 ml) of heated milk and ¼ pint (150 ml) of single cream, stirring all the time. Finally roll 1 oz (25 g) of butter into small knobs and drop them into the soup, so that they just melt. Stir and serve.

A little grated nutmeg can be sprinkled on the surface, but that is optional.

POTAGE D'ARTICHAUTS À LA PROVENÇALE

Blend 1 lb (450 g) of cooked Jerusalem artichokes with their stock into a thick soup. To this add:

1 lb (450 g) tomatoes
1 head of garlic
1 chopped onion
2 tbsp olive oil
handful of chopped parsley

Peel the skins from the tomatoes and the garlic cloves, after pouring boiling water over them. The head of garlic may have 10 large cloves or 30 small ones; it doesn't matter – the artichoke flavour will still predominate. Chop the tomatoes and onion; crush the garlic. *Sauté* them all in olive oil for a few moments, then add 1½ pints (900 ml) of boiling water. Season and let simmer for 30 minutes. Add the blended artichoke soup and, just before serving, sprinkle with the parsley.

SUMMER HERB SOUP

1 lb (450 g) chopped leeks
4 chopped sticks celery
1 lb (450 g) mixed shredded raw lettuce and spinach leaves
¼ pt (150 ml) olive oil
2 pt (1·1 l) boiling water
salt and pepper
juice and zest of 1 lemon
handful each of chopped parsley, mint, basil and sorrel

Pour the olive oil into a pan, drop in the leeks, celery, lettuce and spinach, cover the pan and let the vegetables cook slowly in the oil for 5 minutes. Add the water, the seasoning and the lemon juice and zest. Let it simmer on top of the stove for a further 20 minutes. Allow to cool, then blend. Before reheating, add the herbs. This is a pleasantly green soup, speckled with the darker green of the herbs.

AVGOLÉMONO

This is a vegetarian version of the classic Greek soup. Instead of chicken stock, use the *White Vegetable Stock*.

2 pt (1·1 l) *White Vegetable Stock* (see page 45)
2 oz (50 g) rice
olive oil
3 egg yolks
juice and zest of 2 lemons
salt and pepper
chopped parsley or chives

Sauté the rice in a little olive oil, stirring all the time so that the rice does not stick, until it has absorbed the oil. Have the stock heated, pour it over the rice and simmer it for 8 minutes.

In a basin, beat the egg yolks with the lemon juice and zest. Stir a little of the hot soup into the egg mixture, then pour it into the rest of the soup in the saucepan. Season, and sprinkle with the parsley and chives before serving.

POTAGE DE CHOU AÏLLADE

1 sliced white cabbage
2 oz (50 g) butter
3 pt (1·75 l) boiling water
salt and pepper
Aïllade Sauce (see page 29)
a little chopped fresh basil

This delicious soup does demand fresh basil for the *aïllade*; no other fresh herb will do. If you have the herb, the soup is simplicity itself.

Slice the cabbage and *sauté* it in the butter for a few minutes, stirring all the time. Add the water and a little salt and pepper. Simmer for 20 minutes. Allow it to cool, then blend it, though this is optional. Some might prefer to distinguish the cabbage in the soup. I like a smooth soup, in which the cabbage has completely amalgamated with the *aïllade*.

Reheat the cabbage liquid and slowly add the *aïllade*, stirring it in all the time. It will now turn the colour of varnished oak. Sprinkle it with the basil.

Optionally, you may serve the *aïllade* separately at the table.

GARLIC SOUP (SOUPE À L'AIL)*

There are many variations on this soup.

2–3 heads of garlic (or 100 cloves)
3 tbsp olive oil
2 egg yolks
salt and pepper

Break up the heads of garlic into separate cloves. Pour boiling water over them and leave them in it for a minute. Pour off the water and peel the skins from the garlic. It does not alter the final flavour if you use 100 or 200 cloves of garlic, although the larger number might well affect the purgative, medicinal effect on the body (see page 214).

Sauté the garlic cloves in the olive oil for 2–3 minutes, then add the seasoning and 2 pints (1·1 l) of boiling water. Let it simmer for 1 hour. Leave to cool, then put the mixture into the blender.

Put the egg yolks in a mixing bowl, reheat the blended soup, pour some of the soup over the eggs and stir well. Pour the egg mixture back into the saucepan and heat the soup through, but don't let it boil. Serve it at once, garnished, if you wish, with some chopped parsley and *croûtons*.

1 **Garlic Soup with Saffron and Potatoes**
Make as for *Garlic Soup*, but omit the egg yolks. After blending the garlic and its liquid, return the soup to the saucepan with 3 peeled and diced potatoes and a pinch of saffron. Simmer for another 20 minutes, so that the potatoes are tender. Sprinkle with chopped parsley and serve.

2 **Garlic Soup with Fresh Herbs**
Make this too as for the *Garlic Soup*, but add to the olive oil and the garlic cloves ¼ teaspoon each of crushed bay leaf, sage and thyme, and ½ teaspoon of oregano. Simmer for the same amount of time, blend, then add the egg yolks.

3 **Garlic Soup with Poached Eggs**
After blending the *Garlic Soup*, reheat it until just simmering. Carefully break an egg for each person into the

* It is my contention that this soup does not make the breath smell of garlic.

soup, and poach them in it. Toast a piece of bread for each egg, put the toast in individual soup bowls, pour the soup over and slide the poached egg on top of the toast. Garnish with chopped parsley and a little grated Parmesan.

PESTO SOUP

½ lb (225 g) dried haricot beans
½ lb (225 g) diced carrots
½ lb (225 g) diced potatoes
½ lb (225 g) French or runner beans
salt and pepper
2 oz (50 g) vermicelli or broken spaghetti
6 tbsp *Pesto Sauce* (see page 29)
grated Parmesan

Pour boiling water over the haricot beans and let them soak for an hour, changing the water three times. Drain the water from them and boil them in 3 pints (1·75 l) of water for 45 minutes. Add the carrots, potatoes, French or runner beans (broken into 1-inch lengths) and the seasoning. Simmer for another 30 minutes, add the pasta and continue simmering for 10 minutes more.

Take the pan from the heat and beat in the *Pesto Sauce*, then return it to the heat for a moment. Before serving, sprinkle some Parmesan over the surface. It is a filling but very delicious soup.

CREAM OF CAULIFLOWER SOUP

1 cauliflower
1 pt (600 ml) *White Vegetable Stock* (see page 45)
salt and pepper
½ pt (300 ml) milk
2 egg yolks
½ pt (300 ml) single cream

Break up the cauliflower florets into small pieces and chop the stalks. Boil both in the stock for about 15 minutes. Season it, then let it get cool. Blend the mixture to a thin *purée*, add in the milk. Reheat the soup. Mix the egg yolks with the single cream in a bowl, add the hot (but not boiling) soup to the egg-yolk mixture, stir well, then return it to the pan and reheat, without letting it quite boil. The soup should thicken to a rich cream.

CARROT SOUP

Chop 1 lb (450 g) of carrots and boil them in 2 pints (1·1 l) of *Brown Vegetable Stock* (see page 45) for about 30 minutes. Let them cool and then reduce them with the stock in the blender to a thin *purée*. If the stock is good, then the soup needs no other flavouring.

CREAM OF GREEN PEA SOUP

1 lb (450 g) fresh peas in their pods
1 Cos or Density lettuce
1 pt (600 ml) boiling water
4 oz (100 g) butter
salt and pepper
½ pt (300 ml) single cream

Shell the peas, take off the outer leaves of the lettuce and cook these with the pea pods in the water for 15 minutes. Leave the mixture to cool. Mash it with a potato masher, then sieve it and throw away the pulp.

Simmer the peas and the lettuce heart in the butter for 10 minutes in a pan with a tight-fitting lid. Add the hot liquid from the pods, season and cook until the peas are tender. Leave to cool, then put the mixture into the blender and liquidize. Return the *purée* to the pan and reheat it, adding the cream at the last moment.

MUSHROOM SOUP

1 lb (450 g) mushrooms
1 thick slice of bread
2 pt (101 l) *White Vegetable Stock* (see page 45)
3 oz (75 g) butter
2 crushed cloves of garlic
pinch of nutmeg
salt and pepper
handful of chopped parsley
¼ pt (150 ml) single cream

Place the slice of bread in a shallow bowl and pour a little of the cold stock over it.

Wash the mushrooms and slice them thinly with their stalks. *Sauté* them in the butter with the garlic, nutmeg, seasoning and half the parsley. Leave the pan over a low heat for several minutes with the lid on, and the mushrooms will soften in their own juices. Now add the bread, stirring it in so that it disintegrates. Add the rest of the stock and cook for a further 5 minutes. Leave it to cool, then blend. It should have a thin consistency. Reheat, and add the cream and the rest of the parsley.

CELESTIAL SOUP

Many of the soups that have come to us from China are clear and light. This one is drunk from a bowl with the meal or between courses, and may clear the sinuses if not the mind.

3 sliced cloves of garlic
1 sliced ginger root (about 2 oz or 50 g)
3 sliced spring onions
1 tbsp sesame or peanut oil
1½ pt (900 ml) boiling water
2 tbsp soy sauce
1 tsp seasoned seaweed*
½ tsp kelp powder*
salt and pepper

Sauté the garlic, ginger root and spring onions in the oil, put a lid on the pan and leave it over a low heat for 10 minutes. Pour the water into the pan with the soy sauce, seaweed and kelp powder and boil for 15 minutes. Allow to cool. You can leave it for a day in the refrigerator to allow the flavours to permeate the liquid. Before serving, pour the liquid through a fine sieve. Discard the vegetables and spices, heat the liquid and serve.

A still stronger soup can be made if, instead of the boiling water, you use the clear liquid from the *Garlic Soup* which is left when the oil and the garlic have floated to the top (see page 51).

* Chinese stores sell a wide range of spices and seasonings. These are but two which I find helpful.

CHINESE VEGETABLE SOUP

3 sticks of celery
2 carrots
¼ lb (100 g) mushrooms
vegetable oil
1 tsp seasoned seaweed
½ tsp kelp powder
1 pt (600 ml) clear garlic liquid (see page 51)
¼ pt (150 ml) soy sauce
chopped parsley or chives

Cut the celery and the carrots diagonally into *julienne* strips. The mushrooms can be cut downwards with their stalks on. *Sauté* the celery and the carrots for a few moments in the oil over a low heat, so that they soak up some of the oil but do not brown. Stir in the seasoned seaweed and kelp powder, then add the clear garlic liquid and the soy sauce. Let it boil for 3 minutes. Add the mushrooms and cook for another minute. The soup is now ready. It should be a clear dark liquid with the vegetables floating in it. They should be cooked *al dente* – crisp to the bite. Garnish with the parsley or chives.

1 Chinese Vegetable Soup with Egg
The same as above, but have 2 beaten eggs ready. After the mushrooms have been added to the saucepan, pour in the eggs in a thin stream, beating with a fork as you do so. The egg will cook in strands. Garnish with the same herbs.

CLEAR KOMBU SOUP

Kombu is a variety of seaweed that most health food shops stock. With other seaweeds, it is much used in the Far East in soups and as a vegetable. It is economical, because each strand swells up in the soaking, and its flavour is pervasive though not as strong as one might think. All seaweeds are rich in mineral content, and some contain as much protein as the pulses. Two strands of *kombu* will be plenty to give this soup its distinctive flavour.

Soak the strands in 1 pint (600 ml) of water for an hour, when they will have enlarged to four times their dried size, then simmer them in their water for half an hour. Allow them to cool, take out the strands and cut them into *julienne* strips. Prepare the following:

2 onions
2 peeled carrots
1 green pepper

Slice the onions very thinly and allow them to soak in the *kombu* stock with the strips of seaweed. If you have a *mandoline*, use this for slicing the carrots, so that they are also very thin; if not, then slice them with a sharp knife into almost transparent wafers. Slice the green pepper, put it into the blender with a little water and reduce it to shredded bits. Add the pepper and carrots to the rest of the soup and reheat it, simmering it for a minute, so that the vegetables are hot but still almost raw.

The flavour of the basic *kombu* stock is stronger and pleasanter if it is made a day before and kept in the refrigerator.

CELERY SOUP

1 chopped head of celery
2 chopped onions
2 oz (50 g) butter
salt and pepper
2 pt (1·1 l) boiling water
1 glass dry sherry
2 egg yolks
½ pt (300 ml) single cream

Sauté the celery and the onions in the butter with the seasoning for 10 minutes, then add the boiling water. Simmer for 30 minutes. Cool, then blend it in a liquidizer. Add the sherry and reheat. Mix the egg yolks with the cream, add the hot but not boiling soup, stir, then pour the soup back into the saucepan and stir over a low heat until it thickens a little.

SORREL SOUP

1 lb (450 g) sorrel leaves
2 oz (50 g) butter
salt and pepper
1 pt (600 ml) *White Vegetable Stock* (see page 45)
¼ pt (150 ml) cream

Shred the sorrel leaves, melt the butter in a saucepan and gently cook the leaves with seasoning for 5 minutes. Leave it to cool. Put the stock into the blender with the sorrel and the butter, and mix well together into a light *purée*, which should be the colour of ripe gooseberries. Return it to the saucepan and heat again, adding the cream at the last moment.

BEETROOT AND GINGER SOUP

1 lb (450 g) raw beetroots
½ sliced white cabbage
10 crushed cloves of garlic
2 oz (50 g) grated ginger root
salt and pepper
sour cream

Peel and slice the beetroots and lay them in a casserole dish, with the cabbage, garlic and ginger root. Cover with boiling water to about an inch and a half above the vegetables. Season them, and place in a medium oven on the low rack; let them cook slowly for 2½ hours. Take the dish from the oven, allow the mixture to cool and pour off the stock. You will have a clear red liquid with a pungent and delicious flavour. Throw away the vegetables, as all their goodness will have gone into the stock. Serve the soup with sour cream.

BORSCH

Hot or cold, this is a magnificent soup. I learnt the recipe in Vienna from a Hungarian countess who had been taught it by the family cook in Budapest soon after the First World War. That soup was made with a meat stock, but the beetroot is so powerful that omitting the meat flavours does not harm the soup in the least. There may seem to be a conflicting amount of different vegetables in this recipe, but I assure you that it works. And any other recipes that I have since tried merely emphasize the superiority of this one.

1 lb (450 g) raw beetroots
2 large sliced onions
2 sliced carrots
2 sliced celery hearts
1 sliced turnip
1 sliced parsnip
1 oz (25 g) butter
3 pt (1·75 l) boiling water
juice of 1 lemon
salt and pepper
sour cream or yoghurt

Peel the beetroots and cut them into small dice. They take a long time to cook, and this allows them to do so in the same time as the other vegetables. Don't try grating them, as some recipes suggest, because for some odd reason the grated beetroots won't pulp as readily as the cubed ones. Also, if you come across a beetroot which obviously has a hard fibrous core, cut around it and throw away the middle.

Sauté all the vegetables together in the butter (but omit this stage if having the soup cold). Add the boiling water, the lemon juice, a little salt and some freshly-ground black pepper. Let the vegetables simmer for 2 hours or until the cubes of beetroot are soft. Allow the soup to cool, then pour it into the blender. If it becomes too thick when blended, add a little more water, but remember that it will become thinner when reheated.

Sometimes the cardinal purple of the beetroots goes a little brown, and on other occasions it turns a reddish-brown, which does not look so appealing. If this happens, grate another beetroot and suspend it in a muslin bag in the saucepan for a few hours or until it colours the rest of the soup. This also helps the flavour. After reheating, serve the soup with sour cream or yoghurt or a mixture of both.

Other recipes add a cup of tomato *purée*, a tin of tomatoes or the juice of several oranges. These change the soup into something quite else.

ONION SOUP

For this, the onions need long, slow cooking in a thick-bottomed saucepan with a close-fitting lid.

2 lb (1 kg) thinly sliced onions
2 oz (50 g) butter
2 tbsp olive oil
salt and pepper
pinch of brown sugar
1 oz (25 g) flour
4 pt (2·2 l) boiling water
2 wine glasses dry vermouth, sherry or white wine
slices of French bread
1 tbsp brandy
½ lb (225 g) grated Parmesan

Melt the butter and the oil in a saucepan and let the onions soften in it over a gentle heat for about 15 minutes. Add the seasoning and the sugar, and let them continue to cook for half an hour. Then add the flour and mix it well, stirring continually for another few minutes to ensure that the flour is cooked and has not stuck to the pan. Add the boiling water and the vermouth, sherry or white wine. Replace the lid and let the soup simmer for 45 minutes more. Taste it and correct the seasoning.

Before serving, toast the bread, add the brandy to the soup, pour it into individual bowls, top each serving with a piece of toast and cover it with the Parmesan.

WATERCRESS SOUP

In the classic French recipe, the watercress is cooked for 5 minutes. I prefer my version, in which it is virtually raw.

1 large bunch of watercress
1 pt (600 ml) milk
½ lb (225 g) potatoes
½ lb (225 g) onions
2 crushed cloves of garlic
2 oz (50 g) butter
1 pt (600 ml) boiling water
salt and pepper
¼ pt (150 ml) cream

Wash the cress and discard any yellow leaves, then put it with all its stems into the blender with the milk. Blend until the watercress has disintegrated.

Peel and dice the potatoes, slice the onions and *sauté* both in the butter and with the garlic, for 3 minutes. Add the water to these vegetables and cook for 15 minutes or until the potatoes are soft. Season and leave to cool. Then blend until it is a thick amalgam. Add the milk and the watercress. Before serving, reheat the soup and finally add the cream. If it is to be eaten cold, then use olive oil instead of the butter and add more cream.

SPINACH SOUP

1 lb (450 g) fresh spinach (frozen is no good for this soup)
2 oz (50 g) butter plus a little extra
1 tbsp flour
1 pt (600 ml) milk
2 oz (50 g) grated Double Gloucester cheese
salt and pepper

Wash the spinach thoroughly. Melt the extra butter in a saucepan, add the spinach and let it simmer for a few minutes, turning it over with a wooden spoon so that it is just cooked. Drain the spinach and reserve the liquor. Let the spinach cool, then liquidize it in a blender.

Make a *roux* with the measured butter and the flour. Add the milk and then the cheese and the spinach liquor. Season it well. When the sauce has thickened, add the spinach pulp and mix well. The soup is better if made the day before and kept in the refrigerator. You may then have to add a little more milk when you reheat it. The cheese is hardly noticeable, but the strong mineral flavour of the spinach has been softened. Keeping it seems to amalgamate both flavours so that it is a gentle soup, though still tasting undeniably of spinach.

1 Leek and Sage Derby Soup

Make in the same way as the *Spinach Soup* above, but substitute leeks for the spinach and Sage Derby for the Double Gloucester. This cheese gives the soup a distinct and stunning colour and flavour without overwhelming the leek.

CABBAGE AND CORIANDER SOUP

To one cabbage, you will need a good tablespoon of coriander seeds. Grind them well, and if their shells are obstinate, discard them. Slice the cabbage and *sauté* it in 2 oz (50 g) butter with the coriander. Then cook it in 2 pints (1·1 l) of *White Vegetable Stock* (see page 45). It will need no longer than 15 minutes – if that. Let it cool, season it and then blend it in liquidizer.

1 **Cabbage and Ginger Soup**
Use root ginger; the powdered kind loses all its strength in the processing. Peel and grate 2 oz (50 g) ginger root, then proceed as for *Cabbage and Coriander Soup*, substituting the ginger root for the coriander. This is hot and aromatic, and is best served with sour cream.

BRUSSELS SPROUT AND CHESTNUT SOUP

Use ¼ lb (100 g) of dried chestnuts to 1 lb (450 g) of sprouts. Scald the chestnuts and soak them for an hour. Wash the sprouts and discard any damaged or yellow leaves.

Cook the chestnuts until they are soft, which will take an hour, then go over them with care, because the skins sometimes adhere to their wrinkled surface. Remove any skin; reheat the chestnuts and add the sprouts, salt, pepper and a little butter. Let them all *sauté* for a moment or two before adding the water that the chestnuts have cooked in. The sprouts will soften quickly – leave them to simmer for 10 minutes, but no more. Then cool the mixture and blend it. The chestnuts give a creamy texture to the soup without overpowering the sprouts. The two flavours should fuse, so that neither dominates.

1 **Brussels Sprout and Walnut Soup**
Alternatively, ¼ lb (100 g) of chopped walnuts can be substituted for the chestnuts and *sautéed* in the butter with the 1 lb (450 g) of sprouts. Then add a pint (600 ml) of boiling water and allow the mixture to simmer for 10 minutes. Blend as above when cool. In this soup, the taste of the nuts can sometimes overpower the Brussels sprouts, so judge by tasting.

LEEK AND POTATO SOUP

Crème Vichyssoise, the iced version, was created by a French chef in America, and it has deservedly become a classic soup. The hot version is just as good, for the potato becomes permeated with the flavour of the leek. Though the soup stems from the *potage bonne femme* of the French housewife, I will not adulterate it with the addition of an onion. This is pure leek and potato.

1 lb (450 g) leeks
½ lb (225 g) potatoes
2 oz (50 g) butter
2 pt (1·1 l) boiling water
¼ pt (150 ml) cream

Wash and slice the leeks as on page 22. Peel and dice the potatoes. Melt the butter in a saucepan and in it *sauté* the vegetables for a moment. Add the seasoning and the boiling water, and allow it to cook for 20 minutes or until the potatoes are soft (which may be less). Cool the mixture and blend it to a *purée*. When reheating it, add the cream at the last moment and watch carefully so that it does not curdle. Two egg yolks may be used instead of the cream to enrich the soup, but they must be added with the greatest care and watched with as much attention. It is safest to stir a bit of the hot soup into the egg yolks and then to add the mixture to the hot but not boiling soup.

Iced Soups

Not long ago, I cooked for a few summer months for a hotel on a Mediterranean island. The vegetables grown there were of such superior quality and flavour that one should have served *crudités* only, but this would not have appealed to those staying at the hotel. Instead, therefore, I contrived to devise dishes as close to *crudités* as possible: iced soups made from raw vegetables appeared on the menu every day. The summer was unusually hot, even for the Mediterranean, but the *patron* insisted that a hot soup should also be served. I must admit that I was not too surprised to find that the iced soups were often disdained while the hot soups were eaten. Yet those who tried the iced soups would be converted and would remain loyal to them.

Gazpacho seems to be the only cold soup that is well known. It is also the only iced soup that I dislike, so I am not bothering to give a recipe for a dish to which I feel no devotion. That summer I preferred to conjure up new soups out of the vegetables that were in season and the herbs that could be plucked from the fields. The first three of the following soups stem from that period.

CUCUMBER AND FENNEL SOUP

3 cucumbers
handful of fennel leaves
salt and pepper
½ pt (300 ml) single cream

Grate the cucumbers into a bowl without peeling them, discarding any large seeds, and sprinkle them with a little salt. Leave for an hour so that they lose some of their water.*
Chop the fennel leaves and add them to the cucumber, which can then be liquidized. Add a little ground pepper and the cream. It will then look like a sludge, so add water. The

* This process makes it more digestible.

cucumbers will take 2 pints (1·1 l) without losing the fennel and cucumber flavours, but judge by constant tasting. It is a cool soup, not only in its temperature, and perfect for a hot summer.

1 **Courgette and Parsley Soup**
Grate 1 lb (450 g) of courgettes and discard the large seeds – it is best to core the vegetable first, then treat them as for the *Cucumber and Fennel Soup* above. Oil and vinegar help to bring out the flavour, and the parsley and courgettes should be well blended, so that they become almost a thick cream.

TOMATO AND RED PEPPER SOUP

This is as near as I allow to *Gazpacho*, the point being that the colour is richly red but not flecked with green, which upsets my visual sense, and the flavours are clear without being confusing. Skin 1 lb (450 g) of tomatoes and slice them into the blender without any of the hard core, add a sliced large red pepper, after discarding the seeds. Add a tablespoon each of wine vinegar and olive oil, season with salt and pepper, then liquidize. Add water to the mixture, but not so much that you lose the flavour (if you do, then simply add more tomatoes). The soup should taste basically of the tomato; the pepper merely gives a marvellous kick.

LETTUCE OR GREEN SOUP

Those pathetic lettuces one finds in the winter, wilting in a polythene bag and mass produced from hot-houses, are useless for everything. They have neither flavour nor texture, so reject them. This soup can be made as soon as the splendid Cos, Density or Webbs Wonder lettuces reach the stalls in early summer. Use the central part of the lettuce for salad, and the outside leaves, which are normally thrown away, for this soup.

1 lb (450 g) outside lettuce leaves
2 oz (50 g) butter
½ pt (300 ml) single cream
salt and pepper

If some of the outside leaves seem extremely fibrous, place those in water and boil them for a quarter of an hour, then drain them and use the water to cook the rest of the leaves in. Throw away the cooked leaves – it is no good having a soup which seems to have coarse hairs floating in it. Melt the butter in a saucepan. Tear up the good leaves and simmer them for several minutes in the butter. When they have soaked up the butter and gone limp, add 1½ pints (900 ml) of water. Boil for about 10 minutes, leave to cool and season to taste, then blend the mixture. If you have a couple of spare egg yolks around, mix them into the soup. Finally add the cream and refrigerate the soup until chilled.

ICED BORSCH

Make up the recipe on page 57, but omit the butter. After blending it, put the vegetable pulp through a strainer and extract all the liquid. If made with meat stock, this soup will gel once put in the refrigerator; made with vegetable stock, it will thicken when cool, but won't gel. I don't think this matters; the flavour is what counts. But if you prefer a jellied texture, then use 1 oz (25 g) of vegetable gelatine.

AVOCADO SOUP

The simplest and most heavenly of soups. Take 2 ripe avocados, scoop out the flesh with a spoon and place it in the blender with a crushed clove of garlic and salt and pepper. Blend it into a thick pulp, then gradually add a pint (600 ml) of milk; blend again until it is the consistency of a thin sauce. Sprinkle with a few chopped chives, or sprigs of parsely or mint. The shade of lime green is a delight in itself.

ASPARAGUS SOUP

A half pound (225 g) of asparagus will make enough soup for six, so this is far more economical than eating it plain – if you can bear to forego that pleasure. Poach the asparagus in milk, very gently indeed, being careful so that the milk does not curdle. Leave it to cool, then cut off the fibrous ends of the stalks, squeeze the goodness out of them back into the milk, and discard them. Season, then blend the rest of the asparagus and the milk together. This is no less delicious than the *Avocado Soup*.

CHILLI SOUP

The basis of this soup is the *Hot Sauce* on page 34. Add a green pepper to the mixture and let it cook for half an hour in its water. After it is cooled, the soup can be strained, if you wish, giving a clear, strong, green liquid. Mix this with a pint (600 ml) of yoghurt and season to taste. Serve it well iced, with thinly-sliced cucumbers floating on the top. The confrontation of the coldness of the soup with the fieriness of the chilli is unexpected and must be savoured.

SORREL SOUP

The recipe here is the same as for the hot *Sorrel Soup* (see page 57), but omit the butter. Instead, poach the sorrel leaves in a little of the *White Vegetable Stock*, and then blend it when it has cooled. Refrigerate it until chilled.

Fruit Soups

In a particularly hot summer, fruit soups can be delicious, but they should be tart and never sweetened – the natural sweetness of the fruit ought to be enough. I have had a splendid *purée* of plums, which was effortlessly simple to make. The plums were merely skinned and stoned, then poached gently in a little water with lemon zest. Once cool, they were blended and iced. But good though this was, I prefer a soup which unites fruit with vegetables, as in the following recipes.

CUCUMBER AND APPLE SOUP

2 large cucumbers
1 lb (450 g) cooking apples
1 lemon
1 crushed clove of garlic
1 glass dry white wine
salt and pepper
sour cream or yoghurt

Peel the apples and slice them into a saucepan with the juice and grated zest of the lemon. Poach them in a small amount of water until they have disintegrated. Transfer them to a bowl and grate the cucumbers into them, losing none of the cucumber water but discarding any large seeds. Sprinkle the mixture with sea salt and leave it for 2 hours. Add the garlic and the wine to the apple mixture and blend it to the consistency you find best, adding water if necessary. Correct the seasoning and serve iced, with either sour cream or yoghurt.

CUCUMBER AND GRAPEFRUIT SOUP

2 large cucumbers
2 grapefruits
½ pt (300 ml) plain yoghurt
salt and pepper
fresh mint (optional)

This is a sharper and livelier soup, marvellously refreshing. Grate the cucumbers without skinning them or losing their water. Sprinkle them with salt and leave for 2 hours. Extract all the flesh from the grapefruit, discarding pith and pips, and place it in a blender. Add the cucumber with its water and the yoghurt, and blend it well. Serve it with some ice cubes floating in the soup and if you have fresh mint, sprinkle some on the surface.

FENNEL AND ORANGE SOUP

2 fennel roots
4 large oranges
1 tsp *anise* or 1 glass *ouzo*
salt and pepper

Grate the fennel roots and cover them with boiling water. Extract the flesh from the oranges, discard the pith and pips, and place the flesh in the blender with the *anise* or the *ouzo*. Add the fennel and its water and blend well, then season to taste. The sweetness of the oranges amalgamates well with the menthol of the fennel.

CHAPTER V
Egg and Cheese Dishes

'An egg boiled very soft is not unwholesome', Mr Woodhouse declared in Jane Austen's novel, *Emma*, though he cautiously restrained himself to a basin of thin gruel. Disraeli, in *Coningsby*, is more lyrical, describing eggs 'that look like tufts of primroses'.

The fresher an egg is, the better it will do its singular service. If you live in the country and know when an egg was laid, then you are fortunate. Most of us must buy our eggs from large stores and rely on the store's rapid turn-over and integrity to assure that they will not be stale. There is now a dating system for eggs, but I have still found some which have watery whites – a sign that they have been kept on the shelf too long. It does not much damage their flavour (though deterioration will be noticed if you eat them in the simplest dishes), but it does make beating them into a stiff froth more arduous – if all the whites are watery, it is virtually impossible.

A wooden egg rack or a china holder is important, so that you can keep the eggs in the kitchen at room temperature. By all means keep a store in the refrigerator, but as you use up those in the holder replace them with eggs from the refrigerated store.

One can purchase glazed earthenware dishes with a slit on one side, which enable the cook to separate the white from the yolk. However, some of the white always remains in the dish, and after breaking the second egg, I have found that the white overflows. The best method for separating whites from yolks is the oldest. This is to use the two halves of the egg shell as tiny cups and to juggle with the yolk between them until all of the white has gone. The whites that are not needed on the day can be kept in a covered dish in the refrigerator for some days without harm; they will whip into a froth more quickly when cool.

Marcel Boulestin once said of cheeses: 'They smell of stables, of milk, of cows, of sheep, of Nature; they are bucolic and nourishing; they are a link between civilization and the early history of mankind; they are good for wine, and for cooking, invaluable'. This ends a passage where he points out the excellence of many English cheeses – a point worth stressing.

For classic Italian and French gastronomical triumphs, the two basic cooking cheeses are Parmesan and Gruyère. Other recipes require Emmenthal, and in Italy, the cousins of Parmesan – Pecorino and Romano – are excellent for grating. I would not deny that freshly-grated Parmesan is often invaluable (avoid the packets of grated Parmesan – they are useless), but if we keep rigidly to the recipes using these cheeses, we are ignoring a large potential in the cooking qualities of many English cheeses.

Avoid, if possible, the polythene-wrapped packages of sliced cheeses, for they are cut when immature and have not the pungent flavour of properly-ripened cheeses. It is best, therefore, to find a shop or a delicatessen where the owner respects his cheeses and will allow you to sample them before buying. If cheeses are to be enjoyed plain with bread, biscuits or salad, this is the supplier you need – and for cooking too, because the cheeses will be dry and crumbly. However, I am not going to be puritanically rigid about it, because some packaged cheeses are still well-nigh perfect for cooking.

The best cooking cheese for a sauce is Double Gloucester. It melts as well as – and often better than – Gruyère, and it has a stronger, more pungent flavour without having the sharp briny quality of Parmesan. For complete perfection, I would suggest a sauce which, made from Double Gloucester, has a little Parmesan sprinkled over it before it is put under the grill. Lancashire cheese cooks as well, but is not quite as strong, while Red Cheshire melts with positive abandon. Our own Cheddar is also worthy of respect, but its cooking quality is best seen if the cheese is freshly cut. If you are fortunate enough to get a strong one – the supplier will know – then the resulting sauce cannot be bettered. Stilton makes as good a sauce as Roquefort, and it would be difficult to detect the difference, but it would prove cheaper and the sauce would be creamier if one used Blue Cheshire. Sage Derby makes a delicious, pale lime-green sauce, and if one adds freshly-chopped sage to it, then it is all the better.

A final word on the imported Cheddars: Irish, Canadian, Australian and New Zealand. These differ in pungency and flavour among themselves and individually, for each varies from weak to strong and from flabby to dry from season to season. Some are so weak in flavour that it is difficult to taste them in a sauce, but they are not to be despised for cooking. Check by tasting before using them, and if the cheese is very bland and you have no alternative cheese, experiment by using a spice which can be cooked in the butter before adding the flour for the *roux*. Coriander is especially good with cheese – it must be well crushed in a mortar, and the shells picked out and thrown away. Cardamom too, which is mostly used with rice, must be well crushed to release the tiny black seeds; then throw out the creamy pods.

When cooked with other ingredients, cheese and eggs unite with them in such a way as to change their nature. They should be treated gently and with great respect, for they are undoubtedly delicate companions to the more robust vegetables.

OEUFS MOLLETS

Now let us return to Mr Woodhouse. If by 'boiled very soft' he meant that the white was set and the yolk was runny, then he was speaking of perfection and the basis of a hundred different dishes which use *oeufs mollets*, a phrase with no English equivalent, which means eggs boiled for precisely 4 minutes, so that the yolk remains unset. As they are so special, care must be taken to get the *mollet* correct.

Never use eggs straight out of the refrigerator because that ruins the timing. Find a pan which will hold the number of eggs you wish to boil without letting them agitate in the pan. They should be gently wedged in amongst each other. Have a cooking plate or a gas ring already hot and pour boiling water from a kettle down the side of the pan to cover the eggs. Place them on the heat immediately, so that you can time the moment of boiling exactly. From the first moment, watch how they boil. The water should be bubbling gently; if it is too fierce, the eggs are likely to crack; if too gentle, the whites will not set. For those 4 minutes you must watch the pan. Then plunge the eggs immediately into cold water to stop any further cooking. When they are cool enough to handle, lay an egg in the palm of your hand and with a teaspoon gently tap the shell until it is cracked all over like an aerial photograph of an arid river bed. It is important not to damage the white. If cracked gently enough, the shell will peel away with its inner membrane. Have whatever sauce you are going to use ready and hot. Place the eggs back into a pan with the sauce and heat for a minute to make certain that the eggs have become hot again, but for no longer because the yolk will then start to re-cook.

As they are best served in individual ramekins, an alternative method is to place an egg in each, pour the sauce over the top and put them for 1 minute beneath a hot grill. The timing is dependent upon how warm the egg feels in your hand when it is being peeled. If it is difficult to handle, then the egg may be served immediately in its chosen hot sauce, without being warmed up.

If you are going to have *oeufs mollets* with a cold sauce, then it is somewhat simpler. The shelled eggs can be placed in a bowl of cold water until you need them. The choice of sauces is practically infinite, and I suggest a few, both hot and cold, which are especially good. The quantities given here would serve six. First, some hot ones.

1 **Onion Sauce**
Thinly slice ½ lb (225 g) onions and let them sweat in 1 oz (25 g) butter in a pan until they are soft. Add salt and pepper and work in a dessertspoon of flour, as if for a *roux*. Then pour in ½ pint (300 ml) of milk and ¼ pint (150 ml) of cream and cook gently, stirring all the time, until you have a consistency that will pour in a thick stream. This is a simple sauce, and it is helped if some of the onions are still slightly crunchy. A variation is to bring the milk to the boil with 5 bay leaves and to allow it to cool before taking out the leaves and adding it to the sauce.

2 **Tomato Sauce**
Skin 1 lb (450 g) fresh tomatoes, chop them small, then simmer them slowly in 2 tablespoons olive oil with a

crushed clove of garlic. When they are reduced to a pulp, add as much chopped fresh basil as will soak up the oil and serve at once, before the basil is cooked.

3 **Cheese Sauce**
The *roux* should be thin, so use 1 oz (25 g) butter to 1 level tablespoon of flour. The eggs, being delicate, do not need a pungent cheese; use 3 oz (75 g) of Lancashire or Red Cheddar, or 2 oz (50 g) of Double Gloucester to ½ pint (300 ml) of milk. If you choose Parmesan, then add it to two-thirds of milk and one-third of water. This gives a lighter sauce.

4 **Leek Sauce**
Follow the instructions for *Sauce Poireaux* on page 22, but cook the leeks in butter and not oil. Return the pulp from the blender into a pan and reheat it, stirring with a wooden spoon. The sauce needs no flour; it is merely leeks, butter and seasoning. The flavour is strong, yet delicate, and it is a perfect sauce for *mollets*.

5 **Mushroom Sauce**
Field mushrooms are too strong for *oeufs mollets*, so use cultivated ones and follow the directions for *Mushroom Purée* on page 39 (although the Greek addition of spices may be too pungent for some palates). When you have got the mushrooms pulped, make a thin *roux* with 1 level tablespoon flour to 1 oz (25 g) butter, and add the pulp to it. The sauce is flecked like the best pale but tasteful Harris tweed, and is a perfect contradiction to the simple colours of the egg.

6 **Chilli Sauce**
Chop up some 10 chillies, after cutting off their stalks, and pulp them in a blender with 1 sliced green pepper to every 5 chillies and about ½ pint (300 ml) of water. Strain off the liquid and keep it. Cook the pulp in 2 tablespoons of olive oil for about 20 minutes, then add seasoning and work in a little flour to make a dark green paste and cook over a low flame for 2 minutes. Add enough of the liquid to make a fairly thick but pourable sauce. If you find the hotness of

the chillies too much, you can use just the peppers for a different sauce, but a good one.

7 Spinach Sauce

If the spinach is left *en branche* and a cheese sauce is added to it, you have the classic ingredients for *Oeufs Florentines*. This sauce is slightly simpler and as good in its own way.

Wash 1 lb (450 g) of spinach and cook it without adding any water, stirring all the time to stop it sticking. It will be done in about 5 minutes. Drain away the liquid, squeeze the spinach dry with your hands and chop it up finely. Don't use a blender or you will get more liquid. Make a *roux* with 1 oz (25 g) of butter and 1 level tablespoon of flour, add the chopped spinach to it, then quickly, before it can ooze more liquid, add ¼ pint (150 ml) of cream and stir over a good heat until it is hot.

8 Asparagus Sauce

Not as extravagant as it sounds, because you can use the fibrous ends which no one eats when it is served as a vegetable. Cook half a pound (225 g) of asparagus ends in ½ pint (300 ml) of milk and allow the milk to cool with the ends still in it. Leave it for a day in the refrigerator, if possible, then mash up the ends with a potato masher and pour the milk through a sieve. The sauce is made simply by adding the milk, which will taste strongly of asparagus, to a thin *roux*, as with the other sauces and can be enriched with a tablespoon of cream.

9 Herb Sauce

This can be made from parsley, watercress, mustard and cress, basil, mint, fennel leaves, sorrel – or whatever you have available. Chop up a handful or 2 of the herbs and cook them in 1 oz (25 g) of butter – to my taste, roughly chopped herbs softened in butter are perfect with eggs. If you want a real sauce though, then finish it with a thin *roux* and ½ pint (300 ml) of milk and/or cream, according to how rich you want it to be.

The above sauces are only a sampling of many which suit oeufs mollets. *Almost any vegetable can be considered for such sauces.*

Imagination is necessary, because before cooking the vegetable one must see in one's mind how the fusion between egg and sauce will occur, and then decide whether the judicious use of a particular herb or spice is also necessary. Many of the sauces are lighter and fresher without the use of a roux.

As for cold sauces for oeufs mollets, *all of the ones in the earlier chapter can be used. I find a pure mayonnaise too rich, so would suggest that the variations on the* Rémoulade *are more suitable. Some of the hot sauces are also very fine when cold, though the decision must be made before cooking them. If one is to be used cold, then flour must be omitted and the sauce must be thickened with only butter and cream. Here are some other alternatives.*

1 **Cold Dill Sauce**
Thoroughly pound the yolks of 2 hard-boiled eggs, grind a good tablespoon of dill seed as powdery as possible, then add the dill and the egg yolks to a carton of sour cream. Instead of the dill you can use freshly chopped herbs, but they should be chopped as finely as possible. The sauce, in fact, should be smooth and not lumpy.

2 **Curry Sauce**
Use the mixture of spices on page 25, but omit the ginger root, garlic and lentils. After the spices have been *sautéed* in butter, pour ¼ pint (150 ml) of boiling water into the saucepan. Season and let it boil quite vigorously until it is reduced by a half. Add the zest and the juice of a lemon, then set it aside to cool. Strain the liquid through muslin and mix it with enough cream to make a smooth sauce, just thick enough to coat the eggs.

3 **Green Peppercorn Sauce**
This sauce is very simple and good, and is made with those green peppercorns which are tinned in brine. It is best to buy the small tins. Once a large tin is opened, you can transfer the peppercorns you don't use to an airtight jar filled with salt water and they will keep for a while in the refrigerator. Drain as many peppercorns as you need, rinse them in a sieve under cold water, to remove some of their saltiness, and add them to sour cream.

OEUFS EN COCOTTE

Lavishly butter a ramekin, or *cocotte*, for each person, break an egg into each one, and either bake them in the oven or cook them in a pan of water on top of the stove. In the oven it is easy to overcook them; they can still look quite runny on top while they are cooked much too hard underneath. This is why I rely on the second method.

Stand the full ramekins in a heavy frying pan of boiling water. They will take 3-4 minutes to cook, and it is easy to judge when they are done. Usually they are served with a little cream poured over them, which will warm through in under a minute. Other additions can be made: *oeufs en cocotte pascal*, for example, uses fresh parsley, tarragon, chives, mustard and cream.

I don't wish to disparage *oeufs en cocotte*, which I like best when served plain, but still I do not find them as exciting as *oeufs mollets*. I think that the yolk, being exposed to air and steam, loses the complete purity found in an *oeuf mollet*.

SCRAMBLED EGGS

Such a good hearty English echo the name gives – but they are not hearty in the least. They are light, fluffy and lemon-coloured, Disraeli's 'tufts of primroses'.

You must whip the eggs harder than you would for an omelette, so that the yolks and whites are completely blended. It helps to add a little cold water half-way through this process, say 2 tablespoons to 6 eggs, then season and continue to beat. Melt 1 oz (25 g) of butter in a heavy-bottomed saucepan, rolling the butter around so that the sides of the pan are covered up to the height you judge the eggs will come to. This will stop them sticking; even a shred of curled, crisp egg strikes a dismal note in the dish. Tip the eggs into the pan and stir them vigorously with a wooden spoon all the time they are cooking, which will be only a few moments. Take them off the heat while they are still slightly runny, because they will go on cooking in their own heat as you give them a final stir and serve them. If they are the least bit overdone, they will go slightly leathery. If you are adding *fines herbes*, do it when they are half cooked, stirring them in suddenly and thoroughly. Some of the herbs will fry if you add them to the mixture before cooking, and that is not desirable. Scrambled eggs are delicious served on toast flavoured with garlic or herbs, or with sour cream and chopped fresh herbs.

1 **Scrambled Eggs with Onion and Sour Cream**
Slice the onion paper-thin and leave the slices to marinate for an hour in wine vinegar, with chopped fresh parsley, salt and pepper. Then drain them carefully, mix them with a carton of sour cream and spoon them over freshly-made scrambled eggs. They are astonishingly good when cold, and make a refreshing first course on a hot summer day.

2 **Scrambled Eggs with Green Peppercorns**
These peppercorns (see page 75) lose much of their bright, peppery flavour if cooked for any length of time, so after preparing what you need by rinsing them under the cold tap, sprinkle them into the scrambled eggs half-way through the cooking time, as you would *fines herbes*. In addition to contributing their taste, they look delightful, like tiny green centres of flowers.

INDIAN SCRAMBLED EGGS

6 beaten eggs
2 large finely chopped onions
2 large par-boiled potatoes
1 tbsp vegetable oil
3 crushed cloves of garlic
about 2 oz (50 g) grated ginger root
2 chopped green chillies
1 tsp each turmeric, salt and paprika
chopped coriander leaves

Soften the onions in the vegetable oil. Dice the potatoes and add them to the onions. Stir, then add the garlic, ginger, chillies, turmeric, salt and paprika. Finish cooking the potatoes, stirring them and shaking the pan so that they don't stick.

Finally, pour in the eggs. Take the pan away from the heat before they are set, having stirred them and shaken the pan so that the vegetables are covered with the scrambled egg. Sprinkle the coriander leaves over the dish and serve.

OMELETTES

Most cooks have their own method with omelettes, and much heated argument can occur if two cooks disagree. One must stick to the method that has ensured success in the past.

Your omelette pan should be very smooth, with sloping sides which make it easy to slide the omelette out on to a plate. It is best to keep a pan especially for omelettes.

Make four omelettes of 2 eggs each, rather than one of 4 eggs: largeness makes for heaviness. A two-egg omelette is usually enough for one person.

The eggs must hardly be beaten, merely whirled around with a fork so that the yolks break and run into the whites. Season them with salt and pepper. Melt a dessertspoon of butter in the pan very gently, being careful not to let it burn. Add the eggs when the butter begins to froth, then pick up the pan and tilt it about so that the whole of it is covered with the eggs. Continue to tilt it from moment to moment, so that any egg still unset runs over the cooked part. When only a very little of it remains unset, lift one side of the omelette with a spatula and fold it over towards the middle; then do the same with the opposite side so that you have made an envelope. Slip it out on to a plate and serve it at once. An omelette cannot be left even for a minute without spoiling.

Lightness is the most important quality of an omelette, so it will not stand up to anything but the simplest adaptations, such as the addition of small quantities of cheese or fresh herbs. The following work well.

1 **Omelette aux Fines Herbes**
Use a tablespoon of mixed fresh herbs to 3 eggs. The mixture depends on what you have available: parsley, mint, chives, tarragon, fennel, chervil, sage and thyme are all suitable. Remember though, that fennel and sage are both strong, so add only a pinch of either to the mixture. Half of the herbs go into the eggs as you mix them, the rest should be sprinkled on when they are cooking in the pan.

2 **Omelette au Poivre**
Crush 2 teaspoons of black peppercorns coarsely. Add these to the butter and cook them for a minute or two before adding the beaten eggs.

CREAM CHEESE OMELETTE

3 eggs
2 oz (50 g) cream cheese
1 dsp butter
1 tbsp double cream
salt and pepper

Cut the cheese into coffee-spoon blobs. Melt the butter in the pan. Lightly mix the eggs, pour them into the pan, sprinkle the cheese over them, then pour over the double cream and seasoning. Angle and turn the pan until the cheese begins to melt and the cream to coagulate. Fold over and serve.

OMELETTE WITH PISTACHIO NUTS

3 eggs
2 oz (50 g) pistachio nuts
1 dsp butter
1 tbsp single cream
salt and pepper

Cook the nuts in the butter for a moment, lightly mix the eggs, pour them on top of the nuts, then add the single cream and seasoning. Cook in the normal way.

CHEESE OMELETTE

3 eggs
1 oz (25 g) grated Parmesan
1 oz (25 g) diced Gruyère or Mozzarella
salt and pepper
1 dsp butter
a little chopped parsley

Beat the Parmesan and the seasoning into the eggs. Melt the butter in the pan, pour in the egg mixture, and sprinkle the diced cheese mixture on top. Fold the omelette when the diced cheese begins to melt. Sprinkle it with the parsley before serving.

CODDLED EGGS

These are generally thought of as a dish for invalids, but I find it a pleasing and delicate alternative to fried eggs.

Have a saucepan of boiling water and place a soup plate on the saucepan with a little seasoned butter in it. When the butter has melted, break in 3 eggs and cover them with a saucepan lid. It will take about 8 minutes for the whites to set and the yolks to cloud over, at which point they are done.

SHIRRED EGGS

You need a flat fireproof dish for this method. Melt the butter in the dish over a gentle heat and add salt and pepper. Break in the eggs and let them fry for a moment, until the whites begin to coagulate. Have a hot grill ready, take the dish from the flame and place it under the grill. Baste with a little of the hot butter, watching the yolks to make sure they don't harden. They should be cooked within 3 minutes, depending upon the heat of the grill.

BAKED SHIRRED EGGS

This is an excellent supper dish which can use many vegetable left-overs, such as *ratatouille*, *pipérade*, stuffed aubergines or peppers, or any of the potato dishes.

Chop the left-overs into small pieces (if they are not like that already), put them into a flat fireproof dish and reheat them in the oven until they have just started to cook again. Break the eggs into the vegetables, having made hollows with a spoon for them to sit in. Put them back into the oven for 5 minutes or until the whites have almost cooked through. Have a hot grill ready and put the dish for the briefest moment beneath the grill to just cloud the yolks.

SHIRRED EGGS AU POIVRE

Crush 2 teaspoons of black peppercorns, and add these to a little butter in a flat fireproof dish. After they have cooked for 2 minutes (it doesn't matter if the butter burns and turns black, add a tablespoon of *Brown Vegetable Stock* (see page 45).

When that has cooked for another minute, break in the eggs and let the whites coagulate before placing the dish under a hot grill to let the yolks become cloudy.

SHIRRED EGGS PASCAL

Melt 1 oz (25 g) of butter in a flat fireproof dish, then add the following: 2 tablespoons of mixed chopped parsley, chives and tarragon, 2 teaspoons of Meaux mustard and 4 tablespoons of double cream. Stir them into the butter and cook together for a moment before breaking in the eggs. Proceed as for the above.

SHIRRED EGGS WITH AÏLLADE

Pour the *Aïllade* (see page 29) into a flat fireproof dish. Heat it until it begins to bubble, then break in the eggs and continue to cook as for the basic recipe above. *Pesto* (see page 29) can also be used.

HARD-BOILED EGGS

One has to use the word 'hard' as opposed to soft, yet hard and leathery is just what they must not be. Cooked through and no more is the correct way; eggs left to boil for too long become leathery, and those that are boiled and then kept in a refrigerator for a day or more become much less appetizing after being in the cold.

The simplest method of cooking the eggs through is to place them in a saucepan of cold water, bring it to the boil and leave them away from the heat, with the saucepan covered, until you need to deal with them that day. They are cooked through by this method after 10 minutes. It is effective and less trouble than any other way.

OEUFS DURS SOUBISE

Enjoying what we know as onion sauce, I thought that I had created this dish myself until I discovered it in Elizabeth David's *French Provincial Cooking*. My own version is slightly more simple, because it omits veal stock and mustard.

Slice 1 lb (450 g) of onions and soften them in 2 oz (50 g) of butter. Add seasoning and a sprinkling of flour, and make a paste, allowing the flour to cook over a gentle flame. Then gradually add enough milk to make a fairly thick sauce. Having halved or quartered 4 hard-cooked eggs and laid them in a buttered *tian*, pour the onion sauce over them, sprinkle them with a few breadcrumbs and brown under a hot grill. The same dish can be made with leeks which, if *puréed* in the blender, will make a sauce without flour. I dare say that this is also cooked in France, but I have not yet discovered a recipe for it.

OEUFS À LA CRÉCY

The traditional French recipe uses *oeufs mollets*, but I prefer this dish made with hard-boiled eggs, and I use the carrot *purée* flavoured with orange on page 186. Butter a *tian*, cover the bottom of it with a layer of carrot *purée*, place 4 hard-boiled and quartered eggs on this layer, then cover them with a *White Sauce* (see page 28). Cook it under a hot grill until the sauce bubbles and begins to brown.

HARD-BOILED EGGS WITH AÏOLI

This may sound boring, but it is far from that and is very simple to prepare. Allow a hard-boiled egg for each person and slice it thinly. Spoon the *aïoli* (see page 215) liberally over the eggs and serve. The especial delight of this dish is that the boiled egg is prosaic in taste and texture, while the *aïoli* is fiery and creamy; it is the paradox upon the tongue that gives the pleasure.

STUFFED HARD-BOILED EGGS

I don't much care for tinkering about with food, preferring it to be cooked gently and served simply, but I make an exception for stuffed eggs. Not only are they a pleasant *hors d'oeuvre*, but they are a useful *mezze* for a large gathering of people and go well with drinks because they can be eaten with the fingers. If this is intended though, choose a fairly stiff stuffing and do not over-fill the eggs. Some of the following might be too messy to serve this way.

After the eggs have been boiled and are cool enough to handle, halve them, spoon the yolks out into a bowl and pound them to a powdery paste. Add whatever vegetable pulp, spice or herb you choose and, if the mixture is not moist enough, add a little mayonnaise or some sour cream. The *purées* of leek, mushroom, avocado, artichoke and aubergine are all good, and so are the dill and the *poivre vert* sauces, but something as simple as a teaspoon of fennel, aniseed and caraway, ground up into a powder and mixed with the yolks and a little sour cream is as good as anything.

PICKLED EGGS

'When eggs are plentiful, farmers' wives take four or six dozen newly laid, and boil them hard; then, taking off the shells, they place them in earthenware jars and pour upon them scalding vinegar well seasoned with pepper, allspice, ginger and garlic. The eggs are fit to use after a month.' This is a recipe dated 1700 from Dorothy Hartley's *Food in England*.

Use 5 large crushed garlic cloves, a grated piece of root ginger and a teaspoon each of allspice, cinnamon and crushed coriander. Use a good tablespoon of sea salt with 2 pints (1·1 l) of wine vinegar or cider vinegar, and cook the spices well in a little vinegar before adding the rest of it. The result is a far cry from pub pickled eggs. Sliced in half, with a good mayonnaise, they are a new experience. They are also useful in Chinese dishes.

NEPAL SPICED EGGS

6 hard-boiled eggs
1 tsp each cardamom seeds, cumin, caraway, sesame and
    paprika
a little butter
juice of 1 lemon
½ pt (300 ml) yoghurt
handful of chopped coriander leaves

Grind together all the spices until they are powdered, then cook them in a little butter in a covered pan over a low heat for about 4 minutes. Be sure they don't burn. Let the mixture cool, and add the buttery spices to the yoghurt. Stir in the chopped coriander leaves. Slice the eggs in quarters, lay them in a shallow dish or on a platter and pour the spiced yoghurt over the warm eggs to cover them.

SOY EGGS AND CHILLI EGGS

These two recipes involve cooking the shelled hard-boiled eggs for half an hour, which has the disadvantage of turning the whites leathery. You can get round this by serving them thinly sliced, and they look so striking that I think they are worth doing from time to time.

For *Soy Eggs*, simmer the shelled hard-boiled eggs for half an hour in enough soy sauce to cover them, then leave them to cool. For *Chilli Eggs*, do the same thing, using the *Chilli Sauce* on page 34. The *Soy Eggs* go chestnut brown, the *Chilli Eggs* go green.

TIMBALES

No vegetarian book that I know of mentions *timbales*, but they are very good, either hot or cold, and can be flavoured in many ways. Essentially, a *timbale* is a kind of egg custard which is turned out of the dish and cut like a cake. It is light and delicate, and simple to make. The name comes from the dish it is traditionally cooked in: a round or oval one of fireproof china or tinned copper, with sloping and sometimes fluted sides. It can also be made in a circular mould with a hole in the centre (called a *savarin*, *baba* or the Alsatian *Kugelhopf* – which is what I use). If you possess such a mould, pour the sauce with which to serve the *timbale* into the hole at its centre. Lacking such dishes, you can make it in a *soufflé* dish.

SPINACH TIMBALE

5 eggs
about 1 oz (25 g) finely chopped onion
1 oz (25 g) butter, plus a little extra for buttering the mould
2 oz (50 g) breadcrumbs
3 tbsp spinach *purée*

2 oz (50 g) grated mild cheese (Cheddar will do)
pinch of nutmeg
salt and pepper
½ pt (300 ml) milk

If you do not possess a mould, use a *soufflé* dish or individual ramekins. Butter them well and sprinkle the bottom and sides with some of the breadcrumbs. Preheat the oven to a medium heat (350°F/180°C/Gas Mark 4).

Cook the onion in the butter until it is soft, but not brown. Put it in a mixing bowl and add the spinach, cheese, nutmeg, seasoning and the rest of the breadcrumbs. Beat the eggs into this mixture. Heat the milk almost to boiling and add it slowly – almost as slowly as you add oil in the last stages of making a mayonnaise – beating as you pour. Put the resulting custard into the *soufflé* dish or ramekins very carefully, so as not to disturb the breadcrumbs on the bottom of the dish. Stand the dish or dishes in a baking tin of boiling water, and put the tin in the oven on a low rack. Leave to cook for 45 minutes. The water in the tin should just simmer. The custard is done when a knife inserted in the middle comes out clean.

Let the custard settle for 5 minutes after taking it out of the oven. If it has not shrunk away from the sides of the dish, run a warm knife round the sides. Take a warm platter or plate, place it face down over the dish, invert the whole thing, and the timbale should come out quite easily. It should be served at once with a *fines herbes* sauce (see page 74) or any other of your choice.

1 **Jerusalem Artichoke Timbale**
Wash the mud from 1 lb (450 g) of Jerusalem artichokes, then scrape off the skin with a sharp knife. Boil them in salted water, drain them, and *purée* them in a blender with ¼ pint (150 ml) of single cream.

Add this *purée*, instead of the spinach, to the other ingredients as for the *Spinach Timbale*, and cook as above.

2 **Artichoke Timbale**
This is less strong and is lighter in texture than the *Jerusalem Artichoke Timbale*. Use tinned artichoke hearts, which being cooked lose their slightly artificial flavour. But drain them well after opening the tin, and *purée* them all

with ¼ pint (150 ml) of single cream. Use the *purée* instead of the spinach, and cook as for the *Spinach Timbale* (above).

3 Asparagus Timbale
Use tinned asparagus tips and *purée* them with cream. Again, use them instead of the spinach in the *Spinach Timbale*, above. As this is light in flavour and in texture, it should be served with a delicate sauce, such as a *White Sauce* (see page 28) made with milk in which bay leaves have been steeped, or a *Cheese Sauce* (see page 28) made with a milk cheese (Gruyère, Mozzarella, Caerphilly).

4 Leek Timbale
Use the Leek *purée* on page 22, instead of the spinach, and cook as for the *Spinach Timbale*, above. This is another delicately-flavoured *timbale*, and it deserves a sauce of distinction. Use either the *Sauce Messine* or the *Sauce à la Crème* (see pages 27 and 24).

5 Mushroom Timbale
Use the *Mushroom Purée* on page 39 instead of the spinach, and cook as for the *Spinach Timbale*, above. As this *timbale* is a hearty one, use the *Pesto* as a sauce (see page 29) – or a *Sauce Madère* would be delicious.

Make a thin *roux* and allow the flour to cook in the butter. To this add 2 tablespoons of the *Brown Vegetable Stock* and 1 tablespoon of madeira or a light port.

6 Onion Timbale
Slice 1 lb (450 g) of onions. Allow them to cook in butter over a low heat in a covered saucepan for 15 minutes to soften them, then place them in a blender and reduce them to a thin liquid. Use this as the flavouring for the *timbale* and serve with a *Garlic Cream Sauce* (see page 29).

7 Aubergine Timbale
Peel 2 large aubergines, slice them in rounds, sprinkle them with salt and leave them for 2 hours while they lose some of their excess water. Wash off the salt underneath the tap and pat them dry. Chop them coarsely and *sauté* them in butter in a covered saucepan for 15 minutes. When cool,

put them in a blender with ¼ pint (150 ml) of single cream. Add this to the basic timbale mixture (*Spinach Timbale*, above) and when cooked, serve with tomato or orange sauce.

To make the orange sauce, boil ¼ pint (150 ml) of the *Brown Vegetable Stock* with the juice and zest from 2 oranges. Simmer for 10 minutes, add a glass of dry sherry, then add the liquor to a thin *roux* (1 level tablespoon each of flour and butter).

8 Spiced Timbale
Sauté 1 teaspoon each of crushed caraway, coriander and cumin seeds in butter in a covered pan for a few minutes with a pinch of fennel, nutmeg and mace. Add ½ pint (300 ml) of milk, stir until smooth and let it heat to just below boiling. Then proceed as for the basic *timbale* (*Spinach Timbale*, above). Serve with a cucumber and yoghurt sauce, such as the one on page 26.

9 Curry Timbale
Use 1 tablespoon of the *Curry Sauce* on page 25, but without the chillies so that it is mild. Then omitting the spinach, follow the recipe for *Spinach Timbale* on page 84. As *timbales* are delicate, circumspection is necessary with such additions.

EGGS BENEDICT

The Algonquin Hotel in New York was famous for this dish of poached eggs covered in Hollandaise Sauce, among other things; long after the Dorothy Parker group faded from the hotel dining room, the dish remained. I had it there several times, and it was always perfect.

People can be nervous about making the sauce, as the eggs can curdle, and you need a good double boiler. Try making the sauce in an electric blender though.

3 egg yolks
1 tbsp mixed lemon juice and cold water
salt and pepper
4 oz (100 g) melted butter
hot buttered toast

Put the egg yolks into the blender with the lemon juice, water and seasoning, and turn the blender on for a couple of seconds. Melt the butter in a pan so that it is hot and beginning to froth, then add it to the mixture in the blender while you blend at a fairly high speed. The sauce will become a thick cream very soon.

As a Hollandaise must be served warm, it can now be poured over the poached eggs, which should be well drained and placed on the toast.

POACHED EGGS ON POTATO PURÉE

Use the *Gourmet Purée* on page 153. Cover the bottom of a fireproof dish with it, then put the well-drained poached eggs on top. Sprinkle with grated Parmesan cheese and serve.

EGGS WITH TOMATO SAUCE

Use home-grown tomatoes, if possible. Peel 4 or 5 of them and chop them coarsely. Melt a little butter and olive oil in a shallow fireproof dish. Throw the tomatoes into the dish with a tablespoon of chopped fresh basil and seasoning. Let them cook for about 10 minutes, stirring now and again, until the tomatoes have almost disintegrated into a *purée*.

Then break 4 eggs into the dish. Leave them for about 6 minutes, until the whites are set and the yolks runny. Baste them with a little of the sauce poured over the yolks and serve.

GRUYÈRE FONDUE

Though one can make *fondue* with any of the English cheeses, they are slightly less suitable than Gruyère, because they take longer to melt and to amalgamate with the milk or cream. Also, if not kept warm, they easily become gooey and quite unlike a classic *fondue*.

6 oz (150 g) grated Gruyère
3 dsp butter
6 dsp flour
¼ pt (150 ml) hot milk
¼ pt (150 ml) hot cream
salt and pepper
2 egg yolks

Make a *roux* with the butter and flour and let it cook well for a couple of minutes. Away from the heat, pour in the hot milk and cream, stirring all the time. Add the seasoning, and return the mixture to the heat with the Gruyère. Stir it for a minute. The cheese will have melted by then, and the sauce begun to thicken. Remove it from the heat again and beat in the egg yolks.

There are now various ways of using the *fondue*. It can be the rich filling in a short-crust pastry tart or of a *choux* pastry, or of pancakes. Or it can be used as in the following recipe.

FONDUE CROQUETTES

1 recipe for *Gruyère Fondue*, above
2 eggs
1 tbsp oil
salt and pepper
2 oz (50 g) flour
6 oz (175 g) breadcrumbs

Pour the *fondue* into a baking tray, cover it with foil and chill it in the refrigerator. It can be left for a day if you wish.

Beat the eggs, oil and seasoning together in a soup plate. Have the flour on another plate and the breadcrumbs on a third one. Cut the fondue into squares – the size depends on your appetite and on whether the fondue croquettes are to be served as a luncheon dish, an appetizer or an *hors d'oeuvre*. For the last two, you might want to roll the *fondue* into small balls instead of cutting it.

Cover the *fondue* pieces or balls in flour, dusting it on with your fingers. Then soak it in the egg mixture, and finally roll it in the breadcrumbs, making sure that the pieces are covered completely.

Heat a little butter and oil together and fry the croquettes in it until the breadcrumbs are brown and crisp. Keep them warm in the oven until they are all done.

FRIED CHEESE

For those of us who adore cheeses, this is possibly the most delicious appetizer of all. I prefer the more powerful Parmesan, but nearly every cheese can be served in this manner, including all of our excellent English cheeses, and even those varieties which are sliced and packaged when still immature. A dull imported Cheddar will be enhanced out of all recognition. But one warning: too many, taken greedily, may cause indigestion.

The very hard cheeses, such as Parmesan, can be sliced into 1-inch strips, ⅛-inch in thickness. Other cheeses that melt more quickly, as do many English cheeses, need cubing into 1-inch squares.

Dip the cut cheese into flour, then beaten egg and finally into breadcrumbs. Make sure all sides are covered, then drop them into hot vegetable oil and cook them for about a minute, so that the outside is brown and crisp. Take them from the pan and leave them until cool enough to be eaten – about another minute. The cheese will have melted within a crunchy and golden crust. Ideally the frying is done in deep fat, but I often do it in the frying pan with perfect success.

CHEESE SANDWICH CROÛTONS

Mix equal portions of cream cheese and a skimmed-milk soft cheese with a tablespoon of grated Parmesan, some finely chopped fresh herbs and 2 crushed cloves of garlic.

Slice a wholemeal loaf and cut the crusts from it. Now make up sandwiches with the cheese mixture and leave them to stand for an hour, so that the bread soaks up the herbs and garlic. Use a generous 1 oz (25 g) of filling for each sandwich. Cut the sandwiches into 1-inch cubes and proceed as for the *Fried Cheese*, above. Again, make sure that the cubes are well covered with flour, egg and breadcrumbs. They can also be dipped into a light batter, instead of into the egg, flour and breadcrumb mixture, and then deep fried; this produces a more substantial appetizer.

FRIED CHEESE AND EGG SANDWICH

This is a common dish in southern Italy, and is perfect for a light luncheon or supper.

Cut the crusts from some slices of bread (allowing 2 slices for each person), spread some Bel Paese over them and press them together in twos, so that the bread encloses the cheese. Beat 2 eggs and put the sandwiches to soak in the eggs for 30 minutes (2 eggs would be sufficient for 4 sandwiches) turning them once so that both sides are well steeped. Fry them in hot oil and serve at once.

MELTED CHEESE ON TOAST

A simple, delicious and very common dish. Use Double Gloucester; it melts well, its flavour is strong and its colour is that of a fresh egg yolk. Slice the cheese thinly, put it into a fireproof dish and melt it under the grill. Have ready hot toast which is lightly buttered, and spread it with a little *Meaux* mustard. Pour the melted cheese from the dish on to the toast, easing the last of it out with a spatula. Serve at once, before the cheese becomes too gooey and crisp.

WELSH RAREBIT

This is basically a cheese sauce – and a more homely one than *fondue*. Make a thin *roux*, adding salt and a pinch of cayenne pepper. Pour ½ pint (300 ml) of heated milk on to the *roux* and stir until it is smooth. (A richer sauce can be made with half milk and half cream.) Throw into the sauce ½ lb (225 g) of grated Double Gloucester cheese and stir it over a low heat until melted. Pour this over the hot toast and brown it under the grill.

The true Welsh Rarebit uses ale instead of milk in the sauce – not being over-fond of beer I have never tried it.

STILTON CHEESE BALLS

½ lb (225 g) Stilton
3 oz (75 g) softened butter
2 tbsp mixed chopped parsley and spring onions
a drop of tabasco sauce or a pinch of cayenne
2 oz (50 g) breadcrumbs

Mix the Stilton and the butter into a paste and add the parsley, onions and tabasco sauce or cayenne. Taste, and check the seasoning. Take out a teaspoon of the mixture and roll it into balls with your fingers; then roll it in the breadcrumbs. Continue until all the mixture has been used; chill them in the refrigerator for an hour before serving.

SOFT HERB CHEESE

6 oz (175 g) curd cheese
3 oz (75 g) cream cheese
2 oz (50 g) grated strong Cheddar or Parmesan
2 crushed cloves of garlic
salt and pepper
2 tbsp freshly chopped parsley, mint or watercress

Mix everything together and leave for a few hours in the refrigerator before serving.

CHEESE SPREAD

This is a variation on Liptauer.

6 oz (175 g) cream cheese
6 oz (175 g) curd cheese
4 finely chopped spring onions
2 finely chopped green chillies
1 tbsp capers
1 tsp mustard
1 tsp lemon juice
2 oz (50 g) softened butter
paprika
salt and pepper
4 chopped gherkins

Put the onions and the chillies in the blender with the capers, mustard, gherkins, lemon juice and butter. Blend to a thick *purée* and add the cheeses. Mix well, finally adding the seasoning and paprika.

Souffles

CHEESE SOUFFLÉ

4 eggs
2 oz (50 g) grated Parmesan
2 oz (50 g) grated Double Gloucester
1 oz (25 g) butter plus a little extra
1 oz (25 g) flour
½ pt (300 ml) milk
salt and pepper
2 extra egg whites

Thoroughly butter a *soufflé* dish with the extra butter. For a *soufflé* this size, you need a dish about 8 inches in diameter; don't bother to tie greaseproof paper around it. Preheat the oven to 400°F/200°C/Gas Mark 6. Separate the whole eggs, putting the yolks into a little bowl and the whites, plus the extra two, into a bowl big enough to beat them in.

Make a *roux* with the butter and the flour; use a large saucepan because you are going to mix the whole thing in it. Add the milk, bit by bit, stirring well after each addition so that it has amalgamated with the *roux* before you add more. Cook it for about 2 minutes, stirring all the time, then take it off the heat and stir in the cheeses. If they haven't melted within a few moments, return the pan to the heat and go on stirring until they do so.

Take the pan from the heat and allow the mixture to cool for a moment, then beat the egg yolks into the cheese sauce. (They would turn to scrambled egg if the sauce were still boiling hot.) Season well; the addition of the egg whites will dilute the flavour, so allow for that.

Beat the egg whites until they are stiff enough to hold a peak (there is no point in over-beating). The sauce with the yolks in it can be left to stand for a while if it suits your timetable, but not the beaten whites, which will soon go watery underneath and so must be done just before they are added to the sauce. Put about half of the beaten whites on top of the sauce. Fold them into the cheese mixture with a palette knife, scooping the sauce up from the bottom of the saucepan and turning it over, rotating it each time. Though it should be well mixed, it is important not to squash all the air out of the whites, so work slowly and gently. It doesn't matter if a few streaks of the white are still discernible. Add the rest of the whites the same way.

Pour the mixture into the *soufflé* dish and put it on the middle rack of the oven. After 2 minutes, reduce the heat to 375°F/190°C/Gas Mark 5. In my oven, it will be cooked in 30 minutes, but ovens differ, so yours may take longer. The *soufflé* is done when it has risen to twice its height and is brown on top. I like the centre to be still moist, but that is a matter of taste. A *soufflé* sinks very quickly once it is out of the oven, so those about to eat it must be ready and waiting for it.

The following *soufflés* are variations on the *Cheese Soufflé*.

1 **Garlic Cream Soufflé**
 Make the sauce with a mixture of ¼ pint (150 ml) of milk and ¼ pint (150 ml) of *Garlic Cream* (see page 29). The cheeses should be 3 oz (75 g) of grated Parmesan and 3 oz (75 g) of grated Gruyère. Use some of the Parmesan to coat the bottom and sides of the buttered *soufflé* dish.

2 **Onion Soufflé**
 Use an onion *purée* instead of cheese. Make the *purée* by finely chopping 2 or 3 onions, cooking them in butter for 10 minutes in a covered pan and liquidizing them in the blender. Add this *purée* to ¼ pint (150 ml) of milk and make the sauce with it.

3 **Aïllade Soufflé**
 Heat 4 tablespoons of *Aïllade Sauce* (see page 29) and add it to the *roux*, making a thin paste. Then make the sauce as usual with the ¼ pint (150 ml) of milk – but with no cheese, of course.

4 **Soufflé Fines Herbes**
 Make the sauce with a herb butter. Put 2 oz (50 g) of butter in the blender with a tablespoon each of chopped parsley,

mint, basil and chives, and blend until the herbs are well crushed. Then proceed as for the *Cheese Soufflé*, except that the only cheese you use is 2 oz (50 g) of grated Parmesan.

5 **Spinach Soufflé**
Add 4 tablespoons of *Spinach Purée* (see page 38) to the milk before making the sauce, and use only 2 oz (50 g) of grated Parmesan.

EGG-WHITE SOUFFLÉ

This is a different and even lighter *soufflé*, using only the whites of eggs – an excellent way of utilizing those you have stored in the refrigerator.

6 egg whites
3 oz (75 g) grated Double Gloucester
2 oz (50 g) grated Parmesan
2 oz (50 g) diced Gruyère or Bel Paese
2 oz (50 g) butter plus a little extra
6 dsp flour
¼ pt (150 ml) cream
salt, pepper and a grating of nutmeg

Preheat the oven to 400°F/200°C/Gas Mark 6, and butter the *soufflé* dish, as for the *Cheese Soufflé*. Add a good dusting of the Parmesan to the bottom and sides of the dish.

Make the sauce as for the *Cheese Soufflé*, using the cream instead of the milk, and the Double Gloucester cheese.

After you have folded in the egg whites, gently mix in the Gruyère. Sprinkle the rest of the Parmesan over the surface of the *soufflé* just before you put it in the oven.

Quiches

A *quiche* ought not to be rushed from the oven to the table, because the flavour is best appreciated when it has cooled down for 5 minutes or so. It will subside a little, but that does not matter.

To fill a light *quiche*, use single cream and no flour, and choose a light cheese, such as cream cheese, Gruyère, Parmesan, Bel Paese or Caerphilly. A heavier filling may be made with a *roux* and flavoured with a heartier cheese, such as Cheddar, Sage Derby or Double Gloucester.

PASTRY FOR QUICHE

As pastry stores beautifully in the freezer, it is worth keeping a supply for making *quiches*. The necessary short-crust pastry is made with butter and should always line the dish as thinly as possible. This recipe is for one case.

6 oz (175 g) plain flour
3 oz (75 g) butter
½ tsp salt
2–4 tbsp iced water
a little butter

Sift the flour with the salt and crumble the butter into it. Add the iced water and mould it into a ball. Butter a flan dish or *tian* and spread the pastry over it with your hands, pressing it down thinly against the bottom and up the sides. Cover the bottom with dried beans and bake it in a preheated oven at 400°F/200°C/Gas Mark 6 for 15–20 minutes. Pour out the beans.

ONION QUICHE

1 lb (450 g) sliced onions
½ pt (300 ml) single cream
2 oz (50 g) butter
salt and pepper
a pinch of nutmeg
3 egg yolks
1 cooked pastry case

Melt the butter in a saucepan and soften the onions in it with the salt, pepper and nutmeg. Let them cook for about 15 minutes over a low heat, with the lid of the saucepan tightly on. Take them from the heat, let them cool for a moment, stir in the cream and the egg yolks, pour it into the pastry case and cook it in an oven preheated to 400°F/200°C/Gas Mark 6 for 30 minutes.

For a variation, stone enough black olives to cover the bottom of the pastry case and pour the onion mixture over them. Cover the top with olives, over which sprinkle 2 oz (50 g) of grated Parmesan.

In the same way you can make the following:

1 **Mushroom Quiche**
Substitute, for the onions, 1 lb (450 g) of mushrooms, sliced and cooked in butter until they are soft and are beginning to simmer in their own liquid.

2 **Spinach Quiche**
Use 1 lb (450 g) of cleaned spinach, torn into pieces as small as bay leaves and cooked in butter for 5 minutes.

3 **Endive Quiche**
Use the separated leaves of 4 large endives, cooked in butter for about 10 minutes.

4 **Asparagus Quiche**
Use a tin of asparagus tips, drained and blended to a *purée* with a tablespoon of milk. Because the flavour is delicate, substitute 4 oz (100 g) of cream cheese for the Double Gloucester. Sprinkle the top with grated Parmesan.

QUICHE AU POIVRE

1 tbsp crushed black peppercorns
4 oz (100 g) cream cheese
2 oz (50 g) grated Parmesan
2 oz (50 g) butter
1 tsp salt
½ pt (300 ml) single cream
3 egg yolks
1 cooked pastry case

Cook the peppercorns in the butter for a few minutes, letting the butter bubble and brown a little, but not go black. Take it from the heat, let it cool for a moment, then add the salt, cream and egg yolks. Dot the cream cheese over the pastry case, then pour in the mixture; sprinkle the top with the Parmesan and bake for 30 minutes at 400°F/200°C/Gas Mark 6.

STILTON QUICHE

3 oz (75 g) Stilton
3 oz (75 g) cream cheese
3 oz (75 g) curd cheese
2 oz (50 g) butter
3 eggs
¼ pt (150 ml) single cream
salt, pepper and a pinch of cayenne
1 tbsp chopped spring onions
1 tbsp chopped parsley
1 cooked pastry case

Mash the cheeses and the butter together with a fork, then beat in the eggs and the cream, making sure that there are no lumps. Add the seasoning and the herbs. Pour the mixture into the pastry case and bake it in the oven for 30 minutes at 400°F/200°C/Gas Mark 6.

LEEK QUICHE

1 lb (450 g) leeks
2 oz (50 g) butter
½ pt (300 ml) single cream
3 eggs
2 oz (50 g) grated Double Gloucester
2 oz (50 g) grated Parmesan
1 cooked pastry case

Cut the leeks lengthwise down the middle; clean them and discard the tougher green parts (but not all of the green, because much of it is delicious). Slice the leeks across, diagonally, into ½-inch lengths. Cook them in the butter over a low heat for about 15 minutes. Take them from the heat, let them cool for a moment, and stir in the cream, eggs and Double Gloucester. Pour the mixture into the pastry case and sprinkle the top with the Parmesan. Bake for 30 minutes at 400°F/200°C/Gas Mark 6.

TOMATO QUICHE

1 lb (450 g) tomatoes, home-grown, if possible
1 sliced onion
2 crushed cloves of garlic
1 tsp each oregano and basil
2 tbsp olive oil
2 tbsp tomato *purée*
salt and pepper
4 beaten eggs
a dozen stoned black olives
2 oz (50 g) grated Cheddar cheese
1 cooked pastry case

Peel the tomatoes, after plunging them in boiling water, and chop them coarsely. Cook them in the oil in a covered pan over a low heat with the onion, garlic and herbs. Let them stew for about 15 minutes, then stir in the tomato *purée* and the seasoning. Take it from the heat, allow it to cool for a moment, then pour the mixture into the eggs and mix. Pour it into the pastry case, dot the top with the olives and sprinkle it with the Cheddar. Bake for 30 minutes at 400°F/200°C/Gas Mark 6.

QUICHE AU RATATOUILLE

8 tbsp *ratatouille* (see page 180)
3 eggs
4 oz (100 g) grated Cheddar cheese
1 cooked pastry case

Mix the *ratatouille*, eggs and cheese together, pour them into the pastry case and bake it in the oven for 30 minutes at 400°F/200°C/Gas Mark 6. For a variation, after you have filled the case, make a star-shaped pattern in the filling by indenting with the back of a spoon and fill the pattern with single cream.

Mousses

A mousse may be made in either a *terrine* or a bread tin. It is a cousin of the *soufflé*, but less airy (though still light), so that it does not have to be eaten at once. This makes it a more suitable dish for occasions when you cannot count on your guests' punctuality.

LEEK MOUSSE

    1 lb (450 g) leeks
    4 oz (100 g) butter, and a little extra for buttering the *terrine*
    2 oz (50 g) flour, or a little over
    4 eggs, separated
    salt and pepper

Preheat the oven to a medium heat. Trim the tougher green parts off the leeks, wash the rest well and cut it into small pieces. Soften them thoroughly in 2 oz (50 g) of the butter and reduce them to a *purée* in the blender.

Make a *roux* with 2 oz (50 g) of the butter and perhaps a bit more than 2 oz (50 g) of flour – it should be a thick one. Add the *purée* to the *roux*. Do this over a very low flame to help it amalgamate thoroughly; it is not necessary though to cook it like a sauce. Take it off the heat, let it cool for a moment, then stir in the egg yolks and the seasoning. Beat the egg whites until they are very stiff and fold them into the mixture.

Pour it into a buttered *terrine* or bread tin, put it in the oven and let it cook for an hour or more. It is done when a knife plunged into the centre comes out clean.

The mousse will have risen in the cooking and can be eaten at once as a hot *hors d'oeuvre*, but it is very good if left for a day and eaten cold, in slices. It will, of course, have collapsed somewhat, but will still be very light and moist.

SPINACH MOUSSE

2 cups *Spinach Purée* (see page 38)
6 oz (175 g) butter, and a little extra for buttering the *terrine*
2 oz (50 g) flour, or a little over
¼ pt (150 ml) double cream
salt and pepper
4 eggs, separated

Preheat the oven to a medium heat. One pound (450 g) of spinach leaves will reduce to about 2 cups of *purée*.

Make a thick *roux* with 2 oz (50 g) of the butter and 2 oz (50 g), or a bit more, of the flour. Add to this the liquid given out by the spinach during the first stage of its cooking. Then stir in the cream and season it – it will make a thick sauce.

Take the sauce from the heat, let it cool for a moment, then stir in the egg yolks followed by the spinach. Lastly, beat the egg whites stiffly and fold them into the spinach mixture. Pour it into a buttered *terrine* or bread tin, put it in the oven and let it cook for an hour.

CHEESE MOUSSE WITH GREEN PEPPERCORN CREAM

¼ lb (100 g) grated Double Gloucester cheese or grated Sage Derby cheese
2 oz (50 g) butter, with a little extra for buttering the *terrine*
2 oz (50 g) flour
¼ pt (150 ml) milk
½ tsp dry mustard or 1 heaped tsp chopped sage
¼ pt (150 ml) cream
6 eggs, separated
1 carton sour cream
1 tbsp green peppercorns
salt and pepper

Preheat the oven to a medium heat. Melt the butter in the saucepan, then add the flour and stir it well until it has absorbed all the butter. Add the milk, bit by bit, stirring between each addition until it has been amalgamated. Cook it for a few minutes, then add either the Double Gloucester or the Sage Derby and go on cooking and stirring until it has melted and the sauce is smooth. Take it from the heat, let it cool for a moment, then stir in the cream and the egg yolks. Season with salt and pepper and then the mustard if you are using the Double Gloucester or the sage if you are using the Sage Derby.

Beat the egg whites until they are very stiff and fold them into the mixture. Pour it into a buttered *terrine* or bread tin and put it into the oven to bake. It will take less time than the mousses made with vegetables – test it with a knife after 25 minutes.

Let the mousse stand for a day and serve it with the sauce, made by mixing together the green peppercorns and the sour cream. It is rich, but these mousses will serve up to 12 people.

AUBERGINE AND CARROT MOUSSE

One of the appetizing charms of a classic *terrine* is that when it is sliced, it shows contrasting layers of light and dark ingredients. I saw no reason why a vegetable *mousse* should not look equally interesting. A layered mousse is more troublesome to make, but worth it if you are giving a dinner party.

You will be making two separate mousses, to combine at the last moment, so I give two sets of ingredients.

aubergine mousse:
2 medium aubergines
3 eggs, separated
¼ pt (150 ml) cream
salt and pepper
1 oz (25 g) butter, with a little extra for buttering the *terrine*
1 tbsp flour
3 oz (75 g) bland Cheddar cheese
carrot mousse:
4 large carrots
3 eggs, separated
¼ pt (150 ml) cream
salt and pepper
1 tsp Barbados sugar
3 oz (75 g) bland Cheddar cheese

Prehcat the oven to a medium heat. Slice the aubergines in rounds ¼ inch thick (without peeling them), sprinkle them with salt and leave them for 2 hours – or longer if you wish – to lose some of their liquid. Rinse them under a tap and cut the rounds into quarters. Melt the butter in a saucepan and *sauté* the aubergines in it until they soften and begin to disintegrate; then add the flour and mix it into a paste. Go on stirring until the flour is cooked, about 5 minutes. Take the mixture from the heat, allow it to cool for a moment, then add the egg yolks and the cream, and season to taste. It will seem a very liquid sauce, but don't worry. Put it aside.

Peel the carrots and slice them into thin discs. Cook them in a little water until they are soft enough to mash; drain them. Season them with a little salt, plenty of pepper and the Barbados sugar. Now mash them to a pulp and add the egg yolks and the cream.

Stir into each mixture its Cheddar cheese – it is bland because it is needed for its binding qualities rather than for its flavour. Beat the 6 egg whites until they are very stiff and divide them equally between the *purées*, folding them in as usual.

Fill the buttered *terrine* or a bread tin with alternate layers four or six of them, as you like. It doesn't matter whether you start with a layer of carrot or of aubergine. Bake it for an hour.

This is best presented sliced and arranged on a platter so that all may appreciate the design.

ARTICHOKE AND MUSHROOM MOUSSE

This is another layered mousse which looks more sensational than the first and tastes of mythical ambrosia.

artichoke mousse:
1 tin artichoke hearts
¼ pt (150 ml) cream
3 eggs, separated
salt and pepper
2 oz (50 g) butter, with a little extra for buttering the *terrine*
2 oz (50 g) flour
3 oz (75 g) grated bland Cheddar cheese

mushroom mousse:
½ lb (225 g) mushrooms
2 oz (50 g) butter
¼ pt (150 ml) cream
3 eggs, separated
salt and pepper
3 oz (75 g) grated bland Cheddar cheese

Fortunately tinned artichokes lose their slightly artificial flavour when cooked, but they must be well drained and then washed under the cold tap. Put them in the blender and liquidize them to a pulp – which will take only a second or two. If the blender sticks, add the cream and the egg yolks, but these can just as well be added to the hearts in a bowl immediately after blending. Season with pepper and decide whether or not you want to add salt.

Make a *roux* with the butter and flour, stirring it over the heat until the flour is cooked. Take it off the heat, allow it to cool a little, then beat the artichoke *purée* into it. This must not be done over heat or the eggs will set. Put it aside.

Slice or break up the mushrooms and cook them gently in the butter in a covered pan until they are soft. Pound or blend them into a pulp, then beat in the cream, egg yolks and seasoning.

Now stir into each *purée* its grated Cheddar. Then beat the 6 egg whites until they are very stiff and divide them equally between the mixtures, folding in as usual. When filling the buttered *terrine* or bread tin, start with a layer of the dark mushroom *purée* and end with a layer of the same. A further pattern can be added by thinly slicing mushrooms (stalks included) and pushing them gently down into the mousse.

CHAPTER VI
Salads

Lettuce, cucumber, tomato and beetroot; there is nothing wrong with them, if the lettuce is crisp and the tomato tastes of tomato, but if that is all that the word 'salad' ever means, it does become extremely boring. So let us erase that over-familiar sight from the mind's eye and replace it with a tempting bowl of raw vegetables, sliced and prepared in a way which makes the most of their flavours and marinated in dressings fragrant with spices and fresh herbs.

Most vegetables can be eaten raw; it is just that we have become too used to thinking of only a few of them as salad ingredients. Sometimes they should be blanched, to help the fusion of flavours. To do this, pour boiling water over them, leave them for half a minute, then drain them before tossing them in their sauce. At other times they should be partly cooked, as for the Chinese method of hot marinating (see page 115).

With raw vegetables, a *mandoline* or a *mouli-julienne* is useful for slicing, although I managed happily for years with nothing but sharp knives and a chopping block.

CABBAGE SALAD

1 small white cabbage
1 small red cabbage
2 green peppers
2 onions
2 tsp vinegar or lemon juice
3 tbsp olive oil
5 crushed cloves of garlic
handful of chopped parsley

Mix together the vinegar or lemon juice, the olive oil and the garlic cloves to make a garlic *vinaigrette*. Slice the green peppers and the onions thinly and let them marinate in the dressing for at least an hour.

Slice both cabbages as thinly as possible and treat the stalks with respect. Cut away the fibrous exterior and use the nutty heart of the stalks, either slicing them very thinly or grating them. If you do the latter, add them to the onion and pepper marinade. If sliced, put them with the rest of the cabbage.

Blanch the cabbage (see above). Drain it well, then add it in a large bowl to the marinated vegetable mixture and toss well. Leave the salad for an hour before serving and, at the last moment, stir in the parsley.

CABBAGE AND NUT SALAD

1 small white cabbage
1 small red cabbage
2 tsp vinegar or lemon juice
3 tbsp olive oil
5 crushed cloves of garlic
1 tsp salted peanuts
1 tbsp pistachio nuts
1 tbsp chopped walnuts
2 chopped onions
handful of chopped mint or chives
2 tbsp sour cream

Mix together the vinegar or lemon juice, the olive oil and the garlic to make a garlic *vinaigrette*. Add the nuts to the dressing with the onions. Slice and blanch the cabbages and toss them, while still hot, into the *vinaigrette* and nut mixture. Leave them for an hour. Add the chopped mint to the sour cream and stir it into the cabbage just before serving.

SPICED ONION SALAD

3 large sliced onions (marinated as on page 18)
1 cucumber
handful of chopped coriander leaves
2 chopped green chillies
salt and pepper
¼ pt (150 ml) yoghurt

Slice the cucumber into thin 1-inch lengths. Salt them and place them in a colander for an hour to drain. Wash them well under the cold tap and pat dry with a clean cloth. Drain the salted vinegar from the onions. Add the coriander leaves, chillies, cucumber and onions to the yoghurt, with black pepper to taste. Mix together well and serve at once.

ONION AND KOHLRABI SALAD

Peel 1 lb (450 g) of kohlrabi, then slice them on the *mandoline*, so they are almost transparent. Have an oil and lemon dressing ready (about ¼ pint or 150 ml). Blanch the kohlrabi (see page 105), then toss them in the dressing. Treat 1 lb (450 g) of onions as on page 18. Mix the vegetables together and sprinkle them with a fresh chopped herb – chives, parsley or mint.

Turnips can be used instead of kohlrabis, but the flavour is entirely different.

LETTUCE SALAD WITH GARLIC CREAM

Have a good crisp lettuce: Webb Wonder, Cos or Density (the last having, in my opinion, quite the best flavour). Discard any outside damaged leaves or any that seem too tough. Wash the lettuce well and use your own method of drying the leaves. Just before serving, put 2 tablespoons of *Garlic Cream* (see page 29) in a large bowl and toss the lettuce in it.

LETTUCE AND NUT SALAD

Add a tablespoon of mixed chopped almonds and pistachio nuts to 3 tablespoons of *Garlic Cream* (see page 29) and toss the leaves of a large lettuce in the sauce.

LETTUCE WITH EGG AND NUT SALAD

Cook 3 eggs until just hard-boiled (see page 81). Crumble the yolks and add them to a handful of nuts and 3 tablespoons of *Garlic Cream* (see page 29). Toss a large lettuce in the sauce. Mash the whites until they are crumbly, then sprinkle those over the lettuce. Lastly, add some chopped chives or parsley.

Lettuce is so excellent on its own that this is the most elaborate addition I would allow. Mixed with other chopped salad vegetables, lettuce tends, I feel, to be unsatisfactory. Much better to treat the other vegetables separately.

TOMATO AND BASIL SALAD

If you have home-grown tomatoes and your own basil, there is hardly a salad that can beat this. Peel and slice 1 lb (450 g) of tomatoes, then chop the basil as finely as possible. Make a simple dressing with 1 teaspoon of lemon juice, 1 crushed clove of garlic and 2 tablespoons of olive oil. Pour the dressing over the sliced tomatoes, then sprinkle them with the basil.

BROAD BEAN SALAD

1 lb (450 g) young broad beans
1 tsp lemon juice
2 tbsp olive oil
1 crushed clove of garlic
salt and pepper
2 tbsp sour cream
handful of chopped chives or parsley

Top and tail the bean pods, remove the beans and slice the beans in two. Then slice the pods into *julienne* strips. Put pods and beans into a bowl, pour boiling water over them and leave them for half a minute. Make up a dressing with the lemon juice, oil, garlic and seasoning. Drain the beans and toss them in the dressing; leave it for an hour. The beans will soak up all of the liquid. Mix the fresh herbs with the sour cream and stir this into the beans just before serving.

SWEDE AND NASTURTIUM SALAD

The time to make this is the late autumn, when the nasturtiums are still growing and the first swedes have come into the market.

Pick about 30 nasturtium leaves, with a few flowers if there are any. Peel 3 small swedes, slice them, then dice them into ¼-inch cubes. Wash the nasturtium leaves and chop them finely.

Make a dressing with 2 teaspoons of lemon juice, 3 table-spoons of oil, salt and 1 crushed clove of garlic. Blanch the diced swedes (see page 105), drain them and toss them in the dressing. Leave them for an hour, turning the pieces of swede over so that they are covered and are soaking up the dressing. Then stir in the nasturtium leaves and decorate it with a few flowers – these are edible and delicious. The peppery tang of the leaves goes well with the slight sweetness of the root vegetable.

The same salad could be made with turnips, kohlrabi or parsnips.

CELERY AND NASTURTIUM LEAVES

Discard the outer stems of a bunch of celery; wash the central stems, and cut off and reserve the leaves. Slice the celery and toss it in 3 tablespoons of *vinaigrette* dressing, then add a dozen chopped nasturtium leaves. Chop the celery leaves and sprinkle them over the salad before serving.

CAULIFLOWER SALAD

1 large cauliflower
4 tbsp *Green Sauce* (see page 26)

After washing the cauliflower, cut off all the florets and crumble them with your fingers into a bowl. Then slice the stalks into almost transparent discs, blanch these (see page 105), drain them, add them to the *Green Sauce* and toss them well into it. Leave for 30 minutes; add the crumbled florets and stir them in.

1 **Cauliflower Salad with Pistachio Mayonnaise**
Treat the cauliflower as for the above recipe, but toss the drained stalks in a little olive oil and wine vinegar. Leave it for 30 minutes, then stir in 2 tablespoons of the *Pistachio Mayonnaise* (see page 20) and add the crumbled florets to it.

MIXED STALK SALAD

1 cauliflower stalk
1 white cabbage stalk
1 red cabbage stalk
1 bunch of celery stalks
1 parsnip, turnip or kohlrabi
4 tbsp *Sauce Moutarde* (see page 23)
chopped celery leaves

Slice all the vegetables thinly into discs, except for the celery, which can be chopped and put to one side. Blanch the other vegetables (see page 105) and toss them in the *Sauce Moutarde*. Leave them for 30 minutes, then stir in the celery and garnish with the celery leaves.

JERUSALEM ARTICHOKE SALAD 1

Prepare and cook 1 lb (450 g) of Jerusalem artichokes, as on page 179. When they are just tender – after about 15 minutes – drain off the liquid and reserve it for stock. Toss the hot artichokes in a *sauce vinaigrette* made with 2 teaspoons of lemon juice, to 3 tablespoons of olive oil and 1 crushed clove of garlic. Leave the artichokes for 30 minutes, then sprinkle them with fresh chopped parsley.

JERUSALEM ARTICHOKE SALAD 2

Toss 1 lb (450 g) of Jerusalem artichokes, cooked, drained and still hot, in 1 tablespoon of olive oil, seasoning and a few drops of lemon juice. Let them cool. Before serving, mix in the *Green Peppercorn Sauce* (see page 75); sprinkle the salad with a little chopped parsley and serve.

GREEN PEPPER SALAD

4 thinly sliced green peppers
2 chopped chillies
1 chopped onion
2 tbsp *sauce vinaigrette*
2 crushed cloves of garlic
chopped coriander leaves

Blanch the green peppers, chillies and onions (see page 105). Drain them, then toss them in the *sauce vinaigrette* with the garlic. Garnish with the coriander leaves.

CUCUMBER AND CHIVE SALAD

1 large cucumber
1 tsp tarragon vinegar
1 tsp olive oil
½ tsp sugar
salt and pepper
3 tbsp single cream
handful of chopped chives

With the prongs of a fork, scrape the peel in lines down the cucumber, so that it is ridged in white and green; then slice it thinly on the *mandoline*. Sprinkle it with salt and leave it in a colander to drain for an hour. Rinse the cucumber under the cold tap and pat it dry with a cloth.

Mix the vinegar, olive oil, sugar and seasoning together, stir in the cream and add the chives. Put the cucumber into a small dish and pour the dressing over it.

MUSHROOM SALAD

Wash ½ lb (225 g) of mushrooms in cold water and slice them across with the stalks on. Throw them into a bowl and add the juice of 1 lemon, 3 chopped cloves of garlic, black pepper and 2 tablespoons of olive oil. Leave them for 30 minutes. They will have soaked up the oil and the lemon. Before serving, sprinkle them with a little sea salt and thyme, then add more olive oil. Serve them with chopped parsley or chives over the top.

GREEK MUSHROOM SALAD

1 lb (450 g) mushrooms
2 tbsp olive oil
2 tsp crushed coriander seeds
2 bay leaves
salt and pepper
juice of 1 lemon

Wash and slice the mushrooms, put the olive oil into a pan and cook the coriander seeds and the bay leaves in it for a moment to release the flavours. Add the mushrooms and seasoning. Let them cook slowly for about 10 minutes in a covered pan, then turn them out with the juices into a dish. Pour the lemon juice over them.

FENNEL AND CELERY SALAD

1 fennel root
inside stems from 1 head of celery
juice of 1 lemon
salt and pepper
1 carton sour cream
chopped celery leaves

Trim the fennel root and grate it, pour over the lemon juice and season it with salt and pepper. Chop the celery diagonally and add it to the fennel. Beat in the sour cream and garnish with the celery leaves.

FRENCH BEAN SALAD

Top and tail 1 lb (450 g) of French beans. Throw them into a pot of boiling salted water and let them cook for 3–4 minutes – no longer. Cooking time depends partly on their size; they might be done within 2 minutes. The beans should be *al dente*, never cooked through.

Toss them while they are hot into a *sauce vinaigrette* (2 tablespoons of olive oil to 1 teaspoon of wine vinegar) which has plenty of crushed garlic in it.

CARROT, APPLE AND CABBAGE SALAD

1 grated small white cabbage
4 grated medium carrots
4 grated cooking apples
sauce vinaigrette (about ¼ pt or 150 ml)

Mix the vegetables and fruit together in a bowl with the *sauce vinaigrette*. Both the carrots and the apples soak up a lot of oil, which is why so much is needed.

This salad is very common in vegetarian restaurants, where there may be less dressing on the salad, but nuts and raisins added. Any variety of fresh chopped herbs may be stirred in, and if there is a bowl of *Aïllade* or *Pesto* (see page 29) upon the table, the salad becomes a course in itself.

BEETROOT SALAD

If you can endure to peel the beetroots when they are hot, they are all the better for being tossed immediately into a *sauce vinaigrette*. They may, of course, be diced or sliced.

RICE, POTATO AND BEETROOT SALAD

8 oz (225 g) boiled rice
8 oz (225 g) peeled and diced cooked potatoes
8 oz (225 g) diced cooked beetroot
¼ pt (150 ml) *sauce vinaigrette*
1 bunch chopped spring onions
crushed florets of 1 cauliflower
4 tbsp *Pistachio Mayonnaise* (see page 20)

Toss the rice, potatoes and beetroot in the *sauce vinaigrette* and leave them for 12 hours or a day. The rice and potatoes will then take on a pink hue and all of the sauce will be soaked up.

Before serving, mix in the spring onions and the cauliflower; then stir in the *Pistachio Mayonnaise*.

LEEKS VINAIGRETTE

It does seem a huge pity that this dish is sometimes served with leeks which have been boiled into a soggy mess. If the base of the leek keeps its shape, but is tender, then the rest of the stem suffers from over-cooking. However, if the tops are correctly cooked, then the base of the stem is still fibrous. Steaming is one answer to the problem. Here, timing depends upon the size of the leek and the efficiency of the steamer.

Really though, the best method for successfully cooking leeks is to treat them like asparagus. Choose leeks that are roughly the same width and cut them to the same length, using just the white and light green ends and keeping the rest for other dishes. Tie them into a bunch (after careful cleaning) and plunge them into an inch and a half of boiling water, so that only the bases of the leeks lie in the water. Boil them for 4–5 minutes, when the ends should be tender and the tops properly cooked in the steam. Let them soak up the *sauce vinaigrette* while they are still hot.

RAW SPINACH AND AVOCADO SALAD

Tear ½ lb (225 g) of spinach leaves from their stalks and keep the latter for soup. Then slice the leaves into *julienne* strips and let them marinate for an hour in ¼ pint (150 ml) of *sauce vinaigrette* made with lemon juice and not wine vinegar. Stone and peel 2 avocados and slice them into ½-inch pieces. If they are not firm enough, cube the flesh. Stone a dozen green olives and mix all the ingredients together. Serve with fingers of bread fried in garlic and oil.

Chinese Salads

It is worth experimenting with the techniques of hot marinating and stir-frying (see below), as they add a new range of flavours to many vegetables and salads. Some may consider that in advocating hot marinating I am departing from what I preach so fervently throughout: that the manner of preparation and cooking of each vegetable must bring out its inherent flavour. It is true that hot marinating does disguise the flavour of the exterior of the food, but the quick and sudden heat applied for only a short time leaves the interior flavour unchanged. This brings to the vegetables an attractive complexity of natural and imposed flavours, and seems to me to be one of the very qualities that makes the Chinese method so appetizing. (Hot marinating for vegetables which are not to be eaten as salads can be a slow and gentle cooking process, but that does not concern us in this chapter.)

Chinese cooking relies on two, three or even sometimes four stages of preparation and cooking, where other flavourings and hot and cold marinades are used until the dish is finally served. Don't let these several stages be too off-putting, for the process can be done over two or even three days. If, at any one of the stages, the food has not been over-cooked, it will in fact be improved by time.

Once you become familiar with the methods of Chinese cooking and flavouring, the variations are limitless, and here I have merely suggested a few dishes to stimulate the reader to cook others. However, when using either the hot or the cold methods of marinating, don't choose a wide variety of vegetables; too many cancel each other out, confuse the palate and look less appetizing. It is the dustbin syndrome of food which must be avoided.

HOT MARINADE

This basic sauce is fiery and well spiced, and it becomes a bubbling stock in which the vegetables are partly cooked.

The agreeable and, for me, economical aspect too, is that the marinade can be drained from the vegetables and kept in the refrigerator for further use. There is enough alcohol in it to pickle all the ingredients, and the quantity of garlic that I use is a further preservative for the mixture. This is my version – a much simplified one from the traditional marinade.

1 cup *Garlic Soup* (see page 51), made with 1 large head of garlic
½ pt (300 ml) red wine (the most vicious plonk is fine)
½ pt (300 ml) soy sauce
2 bags *bouquet garni*
1 tsp each powdered cloves, mace, cinnamon and star anise
1 tbsp brown sugar
2 grated ginger roots
½ cup *Chilli Sauce* (see page 34)

Boil all of the ingredients together for 15 minutes. The marinade is then ready for use.

COLD MARINADE

1 grated ginger root
pinch of crushed spices, such as cloves, cinnamon and star anise (variable to your taste)
1 tbsp vegetable oil
juice of 2 lemons
1 tbsp soy sauce
1 glass sherry

Cook the ginger root and the spices in the oil for a few moments to release their flavours. Then add the soy sauce and the lemon juice; take it away from the heat. Allow it to cool and add the sherry.

If you wanted a sweet-and-sour marinade, melt 2 tablespoons of Barbados sugar in the oil and add ¼ pt (150 ml) of cider vinegar to the above ingredients.

STIR-FRYING

This technique is much-used in Chinese cooking and involves cooking foods by placing them, prepared, into a pan with a little very hot oil. They are stirred with a wooden fork or spoon, or chop-sticks, so that they are covered in the oil and quickly cooked. *Ordinary vegetable cooking oils can be used for all Chinese dishes, as there is no need to waste the rich flavour of olive oil when there are so many other flavours.*

For judging the cooking time of the vegetables boiled in the Hot Marinade, it is necessary to remember the categories of hard and soft. Some of the soft vegetables (obviously lettuce, spinach and cabbage would be limp rags) are not suitable for hot marinating, but can be cold marinated and then stir-fried. Vegetables like aubergines, peppers, cauliflowers, peas, beans, celery and broccoli can be hot-marinated for up to 3 minutes without damage, while root vegetables need up to 8 minutes (depending on their quality and on how they are sliced). The pulses can be hot-marinated, when the marinade is treated as if it were the water in which they are boiling. This is a good way of using up the hot marinade, for the dried beans, peas or lentils will soak most of it up, and then you can start a fresh sauce.

CHINESE VEGETABLE SALAD

2 parsnips
2 carrots
Hot Marinade (see page 116)
2 leeks
Cold Marinade (see page 116)
¾ lb (350 g) cooked boiled rice
a little vegetable oil
1 tsp honey
1 tbsp soy sauce
chopped spring onions
flaked almonds

Scrape the parsnips and the carrots, and cut diagonally across the vegetable in ¼-inch thick slices. Plunge these in the boiling *Hot Marinade* for 5 minutes. Drain them and leave them to cool on a dish.

Slice the leeks lengthways in half and wash them. Then, using the white and pale green central part, cut them again lengthways into millimetre strands. Toss these in the *Cold Marinade* and leave them in it for a day.

Heat a little oil in a pan, and when it is very hot, drop in the slices of parsnip and carrot. Stir-fry them for 2 minutes, add the honey and the soy sauce, and fry on for another minute. Take them out of the pan, put them in a dish and leave them for a day.

Boil the rice so that it is *al dente* and separate, rinse it under a cold tap and leave it for a day.

Half an hour before serving the salad, drain the leeks and heat the *Cold Marinade* until it has begun to simmer. Have the rice in a bowl, pour the heated marinade over it and toss it. Then place the strands of leeks into a pan with a little oil and stir-fry them for 1 minute. Add these hot to the rice and toss well. When the mixture is cool, add the carrots and parsnips and mix again. Garnish with the spring onions and the almonds, and serve.

1 **Vegetable Salad and Soy Eggs**
Make this as for the above recipe, but at the last moment add 2–3 sliced *Soy Eggs* (see page 84) to the salad.

BEAN SPROUTS AND CUCUMBER SALAD WITH GARLIC CROÛTONS

Chinese stores now stock bean sprouts throughout the year; they are cheap and especially delicious, whether cooked or raw. Some people grow their own, but I have never attempted it.

1 lb (450 g) bean sprouts
2 cucumbers
2 tbsp vegetable oil
1 tsp soy sauce
2 crushed cloves of garlic
wholemeal bread
sauce vinaigrette

Wash the bean sprouts and let them drain in a colander, then place them on absorbent kitchen paper to ensure dryness.

Without peeling the cucumber, cut it across into 3-inch slices, then slice each piece into 8 sections. Heat the oil in a pan until very hot, throw the cucumbers into the oil and stir-fry them for half a minute. Add the soy sauce and fry them for another half minute. Take them out of the pan at once and let them drain while they cool.

Add the garlic to the juices in the pan with a little more oil. Put the *sauce vinaigrette* into a salad bowl. Cube the wholemeal bread into ½-inch pieces. Cook it in the pan until it is dark gold and crunchy, and add it while hot to the *sauce vinaigrette*. When it is cool, add the bean sprouts and the cucumber. Toss it well.

The succulent rawness of the bean sprouts with the crunchiness of the *croûtons* and the unexpected quality of the partly-cooked cucumber are especially pleasant.

AUBERGINE, SPINACH AND EGG SALAD

1 aubergine
½ lb (225 g) spinach
2 Soy Eggs (see page 84)
12 oz (350 g) boiled rice
flour
raw egg
breadcrumbs
vegetable oil
1 tbsp soy sauce
1 tsp peanut butter

Without peeling the aubergine, cut it across in ¼-inch slices, then cut each slice in quarters. Flour each piece, then dip it into the raw egg and breadcrumb it. Fry these in a hot pan with a little vegetable oil until they are brown and crisp – it will take about one and a half minutes. Do ensure that each piece of aubergine is properly sealed. Take the pieces out and put them aside.

Wash the spinach leaves, pat them dry with a cloth, then tear the leaves from the stalks in pieces the size of a tablespoon. Stir-fry these for less than a minute, add the soy sauce and the peanut butter, and fry it for another half a minute.

Pour the whole lot, spinach and juices, hot, over the cold cooked rice and toss the mixture well. Then add the cold crisp aubergine pieces and the sliced *Soy Eggs*.

Sesame paste can be used instead of peanut butter and can be purchased in health food shops or Chinese stores (where *satay* powder that includes peanuts can also be bought).

PARSNIP SALAD

Scrape 4 large parsnips and cut them diagonally into $\frac{1}{4}$-inch slices. Grate 2 ginger roots, sweat them in a little vegetable oil over a low heat, then put the slices of parsnip into the oil and cover them, turning the vegetables in the oil and ginger for a moment. Pour in enough boiling water to cover them and simmer for about 5 minutes or until they are just soft. Leave them in the liquid to cool. They may need only 3 minutes simmering, depending on their size, for cooling them in the liquid will add to the cooking time.

Drain them and have ready a *sauce vinaigrette* made from 1 teaspoon of lemon juice, a teaspoon of honey and 3 tablespoons of olive oil. Serve the parsnips in the dressing, surrounded with crisp lettuce. The ginger and honey give a glowing flavour to the vegetable.

CHAPTER VII

Substantial Dishes: Rice, Pasta and Potato

These are not only substantial dishes but they are for the most part economical ones (except for the *gratin* dishes and a few others which use cream). Many of these recipes might be the central dish for a large dinner party. The ones that use generous amounts of spices and herbs can be made the day before, then reheated, for their flavours will be enhanced; these include all the curries, risottos and the lasagne dishes.

Rice

Possibly the most economical dish of all, and one of the most satisfying and delicious, is a vegetable curry with boiled rice. The vegetables you choose will alter with the season, and need not be of the highest quality. In fact, it would be a shame to use firm, fresh vegetables for a curry, as their flavour is lost anyway. So use those slightly jaded vegetables which stallholders are selling at a discount. They will probably be happy to give you even more for the original price once you have shown interest. At home you can throw away any brown leaves or cut out any blemishes and you will still be left with ample. I begin with boiled rice and the simplest curry.

PLAIN BOILED RICE

We all have our own ways of cooking boiled rice, so that it is light and fluffy with the grains separate. If your method works stick to it. Over the years I have tried several and the following method is the one that works for me.

1 Wash the uncooked grains in two or three changes of cold water to get rid of some of the starch.

2 Add 1 lb (450 g) of rice to 5 pints (2·75 l) of boiling salted water.

3 Let the water boil furiously, but keep an eye on the saucepan and stir occasionally with a wooden spoon to make sure the rice has not stuck to the bottom. If the water is kept on the boil, then it won't.

4 After 5 minutes bite a grain of rice to see if it is just cooked through. The rice will be cooked in 5–8 minutes. If you are busy, after 5 minutes the pan can be taken off the flame with a lid placed over it and left for another 5 minutes. The rice will then be cooked.

5 Drain the rice into a colander and pour a kettle of boiling water over it to wash away excess starch.

6 Place the colander in a warm oven to dry and just heat through – about 5 minutes.

7 Serve the rice in a warm covered dish.

VEGETABLE CURRY

2 large carrots
2 large onions
2 large parsnips (or turnips)
1 large potato
1 small white cabbage
6 chopped green chillies
3 tbsp vegetable oil
4 pt (2·25 l) water
tsp salt
spices:
3 tbsp curry powder (see page 25)
1 tbsp fenugreek
1 tbsp *garam masala*
1 tbsp turmeric
2 oz (50 g) grated ginger root

Chop the carrots, cabbage and parsnips (or turnips) coarsely, slice the onions into quarters, dice the potato and have all the vegetables with the chillies ready in a colander. Heat the oil in a saucepan or an enamel casserole and cook all the spices and grated ginger root in the hot oil for 2 minutes, stirring with a wooden spoon so that the paste does not stick. Add the vegetables, turning them over so that they are just singed with the hot paste, then pour in four pints of boiling water and salt and continue stirring, making sure that all the paste at the bottom of the pan is well mixed. When it is bubbling and beginning to cook either place the casserole into a pre-heated 350°F/180°C/Gas Mark 4 oven for 2 hours, or leave on top of the stove at a lower heat so that it just simmers. There is a danger with the latter method that the spices may sink to the bottom of the saucepan and stick.

This curry is best eaten the following day, but it will keep happily in a refrigerator for several days. If a hotter curry is desired, use 2 pints (1·1 l) of the *Green Chilli Sauce* (see page 34) to 2 pints (1·1 l) of water. For those who enjoy a fierce and fiery curry, add 6–10 dried red chillies to the oil with the other spices.

For a *Vegetable and Egg Curry* hard boil 1 egg per person and, after shelling them, push the eggs down into the curry and return the casserole to the oven for another 5 minutes. Serve the curry with *Jajiki* (see page 26) and a *Lentil Purée* (see page 36) before the breadcrumbs have been added.

FRIED RICE

Rice can be enriched by being *sautéed* in olive oil before the boiling water is added. An Indian method is to first fry the rice in ghee, then to boil and drain it, and finally to *sauté* it again in ghee, with spices added. But this is perhaps a rather heavy dish for Western palates.

It is simpler to take the warm, dry rice from the oven after it has been boiled, have a hot frying pan with 2 tablespoons of olive oil in it and throw the rice into the pan. Shake the pan vigorously and move the rice around with a wooden spatula, so that the grains are just lightly fried in the oil. If spices are to be added, include them in the oil at the beginning. If fresh chopped herbs are used, then add them to the rice immediately before serving.

SAVOURY RICE

Cook gently in olive oil 2 sliced onions, a few cloves of garlic, a sliced ginger root, a tablespoon of chopped cashew or Brazil nuts, a tablespoon of sultanas, and a teaspoon each of cumin, fennel, fenugreek and poppy seeds. Boil 1 lb (450 g) of rice in 5 pints (2·75 l) of boiling water, after draining and drying stir in the onion mixture and let it stand in a warm covered dish for a few minutes before serving. Chopped parsley or coriander leaves can be added at this stage. The use of saffron does give that appealing golden colour, but it is absurdly expensive. A yellow shade can be achieved by using 1 teaspoon of turmeric powder.

In South India, grated coconut is added at the same time as the nuts and sultanas, but I find this tends to make the rice heavy.

PILAU RICE

If you are an Indian purist, use clarified butter (ghee) instead of olive oil. If you are just poor, use sunflower oil. The *pilau* is baked in the oven, as with a risotto. This recipe calls for a greater variety of Eastern spices than the one above.

1 lb (450 g) rice
2 sliced onions
5 cloves of garlic
1 sliced ginger root
5 cloves
1 oz (25 g) crushed cinnamon bark
1 tsp each paprika, cumin and *garam masala*
1 tsp each crushed cardamom and coriander
1 tsp each fennel and caraway seeds
salt and pepper
handful of chopped coriander leaves, mint or parsley
olive oil, ghee or sunflower oil

Fry the rice with all the other ingredients in the oil for a minute or two, then pour in about 2½ pints (1·4 l) of boiling water for the rice to soak up. You may find with experience that you need a bit more or less water. Place the mixture in a preheated medium oven for 30–40 minutes.

1 **Cauliflower Pilau**
Use the above recipe, but add a sliced and broken cauliflower to the oil with the rice and spices. If a hotter dish is desired, then add some chopped green chillies. After the boiling water has been poured in, stir ¼ pint (150 ml) of yoghurt into the casserole dish. Cover it with a tight-fitting lid and cook it in the oven for the same amount of time as the *Pilau Rice* above.

2 **Vegetable Pilau**
Basically, this is the same as the *Pilau Rice*, above, but it includes a variety of vegetables: green peppers, aubergines, green beans, and thinly-sliced carrots, parsnips or turnips. The Indians always use peas, but apart from their colour, they add nothing. They also use tomatoes, but then the dish implies an Italian *risotto*. It is best to keep it Indian, considering the spices that are used, but these may be varied with practice and experience. Try bay leaves, or mustard or poppy seeds.

3 **Lemon Rice**
Place 1 whole lemon – pips, rind and all – into the blender with 1½ pints (900 ml) of water and mix it for at least 2 minutes, or until it has become a pulp. Strain the liquid and keep it in the refrigerator. (This in itself is an excellent lemon drink for the summer.) To make the rice, cook 12 oz (350 g) in this liquid instead of water for the cooking and bake in the oven as for the pilau. Add lemon zest before serving.

4 **Chilli Rice**
Make this in the same way as the *Lemon Rice* above, but use *Chilli Sauce* (see page 34) to cook the rice in. As this makes a hot peppery dish, it is best eaten with something bland.

KHICHHARI

Sometimes called *krichri*, this is a mixture of rice and lentils. Astonishingly, our own kedgeree evolved from it.

    8 oz (225 g) rice
    6 oz (175 g) lentils
    2 sliced onions
    1 tsp each crushed cinnamon bark and cardamom
    1 tsp each of nutmeg, mace, cumin, coriander and mustard
      seed
    handful each of almonds, cashew nuts and raisins
    ghee or oil
    salt and pepper

Fry the onions and spices in the ghee or oil for a few moments.
Then add the nuts and raisins, and cook them until slightly
brown. Finally, add the rice and soaked lentils and mix well.
Add 2 pints (1·1 l) of water – or *Chilli Sauce* (see page 34) if
the dish is to be hot – and bake it, tightly covered, in a preheated medium oven for 30–40 minutes. The spices can be
altered if you wish; Elizabeth David suggests ginger root,
allspice, turmeric and tamarind pulp.

BEETROOT RICE

    1 lb (450 g) uncooked beetroot
    rice
    8 oz (225 g) sliced onions
    ½ tsp each of cumin seeds, caraway and mustard seeds
    2 chopped green chillies
    olive oil
    salt and pepper
    boiling water
    juice of 1 lemon
    chopped coriander leaves

Peel and cube the beetroots, and boil them with the onions as
if making a simple borsch. *Sauté* the spices and chillies in the
oil, then add the rice and seasoning. When the beetroots are
cooked, drain off the liquid and use it for boiling the rice and
spices. When it is cooked, add the beetroot and onions. Pour
over the lemon juice and mix well. Garnish with the coriander
leaves and serve it hot with a bowl of yoghurt.

RISOVERDI

6 oz (175 g) rice
1 lb (450 g) peas in the pod
1 lb (450 g) spinach
1 oz (25 g) butter
salt and pepper
¼ lb (100 g) pistachio nuts

Choose young peas in their pods or *mange tout*, cook them in a pint (600 ml) of boiling water with a pinch of salt and allow them to cool. Salt them with care, though, allowing for the saltiness of the nuts. Meanwhile, wash and squeeze dry the spinach, slice or tear the leaves into small scraps, and cook them in the butter, stirring and grinding the leaves into the fat for a few moments, until the spinach is reduced by two-thirds.

Mix the peas with their water in a blender, so that the liquid becomes a thin soup, then strain it through a mesh sieve to ensure that no fibres from the pods are in the liquid. Pour some back into the blender and add the shelled pistachio nuts; reduce these to a *purée* and add them to the thin soup. Taste and check the seasoning.

Boil the rice in 3 pints (1·75 l) of water and, when it is just done, wash it well beneath a hot tap to remove the starch. Have ready a buttered *soufflé* dish. Put the spinach at the bottom with the rice on it and pour over all the hot pea and pistachio soup, which should be thick and pale green. Place the dish into a hot oven for 5 minutes.

RISOTTO BIANCO

In the south of Italy, *risottos* are made with olive oil and, in the north, with butter. I prefer oil. Also, in Italy, the dish is cooked on top of the stove, while I use the oven.

This recipe is for the simple, basic *risotto*, and it is an excellent dish to accompany more highly-flavoured ones. From this recipe there are a hundred variations.

10 oz (275 g) rice
2 finely sliced large onions
2 tbsp olive oil or 1 oz (25 g) butter
salt and pepper
1 glass dry white wine or dry vermouth
1½ pt (900 ml) *White Vegetable Stock* (see page 45)
butter

Take a heavy iron casserole with a thick bottom, a close-fitting lid and, preferably, an enamelled inside. Heat the oil or melt the butter in it. Add the onions and let them cook gently for a few moments, until soft. Add the rice, salt and pepper and stir the mixture for a minute or two, so that the rice soaks up as much oil or butter as it can. Then take it away from the flame and add the wine or vermouth. Stir it in quickly or else the rice might stick. Have the *White Vegetable Stock* already simmering. Place the dish back on the heat and add the stock; stir again until everything is just bubbling, then put the lid on the casserole and place it in a preheated medium oven for 45 minutes.

Before serving, stir in several knobs of butter. The Milanese way is to add saffron at the last moment, then Parmesan, but this will depend on what other dishes you are serving.

VEGETABLE RISOTTO

This recipe keeps all the fresh flavours of the vegetables and mingles them in the grains of rice.

10 oz (275 g) rice
1 large aubergine
2 courgettes
2 sliced onions
5 large crushed cloves of garlic
olive oil
salt and pepper
1 glass white wine or vermouth
1½ pt (900 ml) boiling water
1 oz (25 g) butter
4 oz (100 g) grated Parmesan

Slice and cube the unpeeled aubergine into small pieces; cut the courgettes into four, lengthways, then cube each piece.

Heat 2 tablespoons of olive oil in a heavy pan and in it *sauté* the aubergines, courgettes, onions and garlic gently for 3–4 minutes – or until they are all soft. The aubergine may soak up all the oil and you will then need to add more, but if you are standing over the pan stirring constantly, this can be avoided. Season it, then add the rice and go on stirring for another moment. Take the pan away from the heat, and add the wine or vermouth, then the boiling water. Cook the *risotto*, covered, in the oven, preheated to medium, for 45 minutes.

Before serving, mix in the butter and sprinkle with Parmesan.

TOMATO AND MUSHROOM RISOTTO

10 oz (275 g) rice
1 14-oz (397-g) tin of tomatoes
1 lb (450 g) mushrooms
olive oil
3 crushed cloves of garlic
1 glass red wine
1 tsp tomato *purée*
salt and pepper
4 oz (100 g) grated Parmesan
1 oz (25 g) butter

Wash the mushrooms (don't peel them ever), and slice them down the stalks and across into crescent-moon shapes. Add enough water to the tomatoes to make it up to a pint (600 ml) and blend it into a thin liquid. Heat it up and keep it hot.

Cook the mushrooms in the olive oil until they have begun to simmer in their own liquid. Add the rice and the garlic, then the red wine, and let it bubble for a moment before adding the hot tomato liquid. Stir in the tomato *purée* and the seasoning.

Put it into a preheated 350°F/180°C/Gas Mark 4 oven and cook it for 40 minutes. Add the Parmesan and butter, and serve.

1 Fresh Tomato and Mushroom Risotto

This uses fresh tomatoes (by choice, home-grown ones), but as their sweetness can be so easily lost with over-cooking, they must be added at the last moment.

Omitting the tinned tomatoes from the *Tomato and*

Mushroom Risotto, cook the rice mixture in the oven, as above, but in the clear vegetable stock.

Peel and slice 1 lb (450 g) of tomatoes, cook them for a few minutes in butter or oil, then add a glass of red wine (not plonk). Season with salt and pepper, then cover the pan and let the tomatoes simmer in the wine for another 5 minutes. Ten minutes before the rice has finished cooking, stir in the cooked tomatoes and place the dish back into the oven, but at the bottom. Turn the oven off. The rice will now soak up the tomato sauce without further cooking. Before serving, sprinkle the top with a large handful of chopped basil. This is a dish to surprise the most jaded palate. If you have no fresh basil, use a tablespoon of dried basil, added to the tomatoes when they are cooking. Alas, it is not the same though.

BEAN AND PISTACHIO RISOTTO

Though pistachio nuts are expensive (although they can now often be bought more cheaply in markets), they are the king of all nuts, with a unique flavour. When cooked, they have the shade of avocado flesh.

1 lb (450 g) runner or French beans
6 oz (175 g) pistachio nuts
10 oz (450 g) rice
salt and pepper
olive oil
1 glass vermouth
1 oz (25 g) butter
2 oz (50 g) grated Parmesan

Top and tail the beans, then chop them coarsely and boil them in water with a little salt for 10 minutes. Allow them to cool, then blend them, but only for a moment, so that they do not disintegrate completely. Chop the pistachio nuts so that they are crushed but not powdered.

Cook the rice in the oil until it becomes translucent, add the vermouth and a lot of black pepper, then pour in the hot bean *purée* and the pistachio nuts. Stir well and cook in a preheated 350°F/180°C/Gas Mark 4 oven for 40 minutes.

Add the butter and the Parmesan before serving.

KOHLRABI AND ONION RISOTTO

People think of kohlrabi as a type of Continental turnip. In fact, it grows above the ground upon a thick stem, like an artichoke or a very large Brussels sprout. It is usually purple on the outside and sprouts leaved branches from its top. Most markets stock them at the beginning of winter, but they are easily grown here as well, though we appear to have dismissed them so far. They are worth exploring, because their flavour is not sweet like the turnip's, but nutty.

In this recipe, Jerusalem artichokes can be used instead of the kohlrabi, for though their flavour is stronger, there is a similarity.

3 kohlrabis
3 sliced onions
10 oz (275 g) rice
2 crushed cloves of garlic
2 tbsp olive oil
1½ pt (900 ml) clear vegetable stock
salt and pepper
1 oz (25 g) butter
2 oz (50 g) grated Parmesan

Peel the outer skin of the kohlrabis, cut off the stalk and stem, and quarter and dice the flesh into small chunks. Cook them with the onions and the garlic in the oil for a moment, turning the kohlrabi constantly. Heat the vegetable stock, then add the rice to the kohlrabi mixture and pour the stock over it. Season. Cook it in a preheated 350°F/180°C/Gas Mark 4 oven for 40 minutes. Before serving, stir in the butter and sprinkle the Parmesan over the top.

GINGER AND PEPPER RISOTTO

This is for those who like hot dishes that are not curries.

10 oz (275 g) rice
2 oz (50 g) grated ginger root
3 sliced onions
3 sliced green peppers
1 sliced fennel root
olive oil

1½ pt (900 ml) *Chilli Sauce* (see page 34)
salt and pepper
1 oz (25 g) butter
2 oz (50 g) grated Parmesan

Cook the onions, peppers and fennel root in the olive oil for a few moments, then add the grated ginger root and continue to cook for another minute, stirring all the time.

Add the rice and let it soak up the oil, ginger and juices, but keep stirring it. Heat the *Chilli Sauce* to simmering, add it to the rice and season it with the salt and pepper. Place it in a preheated 350°F/180°C/Gas Mark 4 oven for 40 minutes. Adding butter and Parmesan in this recipe is optional. I think this *risotto* needs a bowl of yoghurt and cucumber to be served with it.

WALNUT RISOTTO

¼ lb (100 g) chopped walnuts
¼ lb (100 g) dried chestnuts
10 oz (275 g) rice
1 small sliced cabbage
1 sliced onion
3 crushed cloves of garlic
olive oil
salt and pepper
1 oz (25 g) butter
2 oz (50 g) grated Parmesan

Pour boiling water over the chestnuts and leave them in it for an hour; they will double in size. Take off any outer skin that might be clinging inside the deepest wrinkle. Boil them in water with a pinch of salt until they are soft – it will take about 45 minutes. Allow them to cool, then put them in the blender with the water they have cooked in. *Purée* them.

Sauté the cabbage, onion and garlic in the olive oil until just soft; add the rice and stir it around until it becomes translucent. Make up the chestnut mixture to 1½ pints (900 ml) by adding water. Add this to the rice and stir in the walnuts. Season, then place the *risotto* into a preheated 350°F/180°C/Gas Mark 4 oven and bake it for 40 minutes. Add the butter and Parmesan before serving.

You can omit the chestnuts and use instead a vegetable stock, but add 2 oz (50 g) of grated ginger root at the beginning. This then becomes a *Walnut and Ginger Risotto*, which is also excellent.

CHINESE RISOTTO

10 oz (275 g) rice
1 small sliced cabbage
3 sliced onions
3 crushed cloves of garlic
2 tbsp sunflower or peanut oil
1 tbsp *satay* powder
1 tsp five-spice powder
1 glass dry sherry
black pepper
1½ pt (900 ml) clear vegetable stock
¼ pt (150 ml) soy sauce

Sauté the cabbage, onions and garlic in the oil for a few moments; add the rice, the *satay* and five-spice powders, and stir vigorously. Take the dish away from the heat and add the sherry and pepper. Heat the vegetable stock and soy sauce, pour it into the dish, stirring all the time. When it is bubbling, place it in a preheated 350°F/180°C/Gas Mark 4 oven. Cook it for 40 minutes.

COLD RISOTTO

If any of the *risottos* are not completely eaten when hot, they are excellent cold as a salad. Hard-boil some eggs and slice them into the *risotto*. Chop any fresh herbs you have – parsley, chives, basil, mint – and stir those in as well. Serve with sour cream or yoghurt.

SUPPLÌ

Another method of dealing with left-over *risotto* is to make it into these croquettes.

Stir 2 beaten eggs into 12 oz (350 g) of *risotto*. Take a spoonful of the mixture and put it in the palm of your hand.

Choose a cheese that will melt easily (the Italians use Mozzarella, but Bel Paese would do); the English cheeses are too hard. Place a slice of cheese on top of the spoonful of rice and cover the cheese with more rice, so that the cheese is enclosed in a ball the size of a small orange. Roll these balls in breadcrumbs, then fry them in hot olive oil, turning them over so that they are browned on all their surfaces. The cheese should have melted inside the rice. They are delicious.

Pasta

There are endless variations with pasta, using vegetables, herbs and spices. As in the classic Italian recipes, the use of Parmesan and/or a thick cheese sauce is generally necessary, but as the usual minced meat or ham is so often buried in other flavourings, it becomes irrelevant, and vegetable pasta dishes seem to me more successful.

Anyone who has tasted home-made pasta in Italy will not easily forget the experience. It is now possible to buy home-made pasta in Soho, but it should be eaten on the day it is bought, for it can easily dry out and become hard. However, any cook who is adept at making pastry would find pasta just as simple to prepare, though most of us would find it easier and quicker to use pasta from packets.

It is interesting to note that Italians who keep slim claim that pasta is not fattening if no meat course is eaten afterwards. On a vegetarian diet I have found that I have wanted to eat more pasta than I ever did before, but have found it to be not in the least fattening.

The varieties of pasta made in Italy seem to run into the hundreds, and most of the well-known types are now exported. It is possible therefore to buy both *lasagne* and *canneloni* in packets. Always try to ensure that you purchase the pasta in an Italian shop which has enthusiastic Italian customers; no better guarantee of quality exists.

COOKING PASTA

The one essential factor in cooking all types of pasta is that it must be boiled in the largest saucepan and with as much salted water as the pan will hold. Rough proportions would be 12 oz (350 g) of pasta with 3 quarts (7 l) of water.

Some varieties of pasta take longer to cook than others. Home-made *tagliatelle* will take no longer than 3–4 minutes, while the large shells, *chiocciole*, may take up to 20 minutes. It is essential to have the pasta *al dente*, so that it is just a little resistant to the bite.

Always drain the pasta carefully. It is best to let it lie in a colander and to shake it vigorously, then to put the pasta back into the saucepan with a little olive oil and to toss it in the oil. If you do not use this method, have a warm fireproof dish with melted butter in it and slide the pasta on to this.

LASAGNE VERDE

I must confess to liking more sauce than pasta, which is why I favour the different *lasagne* dishes that follow.

8 pieces of *lasagne*
1½ lb (700 g) leaf spinach
1 oz (25 g) butter
1 pt (600 ml) single cream
½ lb (225 g) grated Sage Derby cheese
¼ lb (100 g) grated Parmesan
½ pt (300 ml) milk
2 oz (50 g) flour
salt and pepper
breadcrumbs
chopped fresh parsley or basil

Boil the *lasagne* in a large amount of salted water, but take care, for the pieces are liable to stick together. Use a large fish kettle if you have one or else count to ten between putting each piece in. Allow about 8 minutes cooking for it.

Have ready an oblong buttered earthenware dish. Drain the *lasagne* and place half of it on the bottom of the dish so that it is covered. If the pieces also go up the sides, all the better. After washing the spinach, cook it in the butter until it is soft, but not a pulp. It should take about 4 minutes, no longer. Drain off the liquid and reserve it for the cheese sauce. Arrange the spinach over the *lasagne* and over that pour the cream, making sure that the spinach is covered. This effectively seals the spinach so that it won't give out more moisture.

Make a *roux* with 1 oz (25 g) of butter and the flour. Add the spinach liquor, seasoning and milk, then the Sage Derby, so that you have a thick cheese sauce. Place the rest of the *lasagne* over the spinach, then pour the sauce over and allow it to seep down a bit, but not too much, for most of it should lie on top. Sprinkle the surface with the breadcrumbs and

Parmesan, bake it in a preheated hot oven for half an hour. The top should then be brown and slightly crusty. Serve it at once, after sprinkling the top with the parsley or, better still if you have it, basil.

1   **Lasagne Verde with Sorrel**
Instead of the spinach in the above recipe, use sorrel – or achieve an even more delicious flavour by using half spinach and half sorrel. Cook the vegetables separately and place them in layers over the *lasagne*.

2   **Lasagne Lyonnaise**
Slice 2 lb (1 kg) of onions and soften them in butter with a teaspoon of crushed caraway seeds. They will be cooked through over a gentle heat and in a closed pan after 5 minutes. Season them and add 2 tablespoons of plain flour, cooking it for another minute over the same heat and stirring all the time, so that it never sticks. Do make sure that the *roux* has cooked through, so that the sauce is not floury, then add enough milk to make a thick sauce.

Pour the sauce over the bottom layer of *lasagne* and cover it with the top layer. Then pour ¼ pint (300 ml) of single cream over the pasta and cover that with ½ lb (225 g) of grated Parmesan or a strong Cheddar. Finish it with the breadcrumbs and bake it for the same time as the *Lasagne Verde*.

VEGETABLE LASAGNE

8 slices cooked *lasagne*
1 lb (450 g) sliced courgettes
2 medium onions
½ lb (225 g) hot-marinated vegetables (turnips, parsnips, carrots, swedes) on page 117
Ratatouille Purée (to cover the dish ½ inch in depth) on page 180
butter
salt and pepper
1 tsp each of fennel and caraway seeds
½ pt (300 ml) cream
flour
½ pt (300 ml) milk
½ lb (225 g) Sage Derby cheese

Soften the courgettes and the onions in butter with the seasoning and the spices. Drain off any excess liquor and reserve it for the sauce. Lay half of the lasagne on the bottom of an oblong buttered baking dish. Put half of these vegetables over the first layer of *lasagne*. Next, arrange the hot-marinated vegetables in another layer and smooth the *Ratatouille Purée* over the top. Finish the layering with the rest of the onions and courgettes. Pour the cream over all the vegetables and then place the remaining *lasagne* in a layer on top.

Make a *roux* with 1 oz (25 g) of butter and 2 oz (50 g) of flour. Stir in the vegetable juices and the milk slowly, mixing it well with a wooden spoon. Then add the cheese and cover the *lasagne* with the resulting sauce. Bake it in a hot oven for 30 minutes.

MACARONI CHEESE

If this highly enjoyable dish is to be raised to a gourmet one, then a little more trouble must be taken over the basic ingredients.

1 lb (450 g) macaroni
½ lb (225 g) grated Sage Derby cheese
½ lb (225 g) grated Parmesan cheese
½ lb (225 g) grated Gruyère cheese
6 bay leaves
salt and pepper
1½ pt (900 ml) White Sauce (see page 28)

Heat the milk for the *White Sauce* with the bay leaves and the seasoning, and let it cool, so that the bay flavours the milk strongly. Boil the macaroni in plenty of salted water until it is just *al dente* (possibly 8 minutes, but you will have to test it after 5). Take the bay leaves from the milk and finish making the *White Sauce*. Drain the macaroni well and place a third of it in a buttered dish. Sprinkle the Sage Derby over the first layer, then add the next third of the macaroni and sprinkle on the Gruyère. Finally add the remaining macaroni and pour the *White Sauce* over the lot. Top it with the Parmesan. Sprinkle some breadcrumbs over the top, if you wish, and bake it in a preheated oven at medium heat for 25 minutes, or until the sauce is boiling and the top is brown. If it hasn't browned, finish it off beneath the grill.

MACARONI WITH SPINACH

6 oz (175 g) macaroni
1 lb (450 g) spinach, reduced to a *purée*
4 oz (100 g) Mozzarella cheese
½ lb (225 g) grated Sage Derby cheese
¼ pt (150 ml) *White Sauce* (see page 28)
2 oz (50 g) grated Parmesan
breadcrumbs
salt and pepper

Butter a *soufflé* dish and pour the spinach *purée* into it. Cut the Mozzarella into 1-inch cubes and dot it over the spinach. Drain the macaroni well, then pour it over the spinach. Mix the Sage Derby and seasoning with the *White Sauce*, when hot, and allow the sauce to slowly cover the macaroni. Sprinkle it with the Parmesan and then the breadcrumbs, and bake it in a hot oven for about 20 minutes – until the sauce is bubbling and the top is crisp.

MACARONI WITH EGGS AND HERBS

This is as good with spaghetti or *rigatoni* and is a vegetarian version of *pasta alla carbonara*. Coriander leaves could be used instead of the other herbs, but you will then have a much stronger-tasting dish.

10 oz (225 g) cooked pasta
4 eggs
2 oz (50 g) butter
a good handful of finely-chopped parsley and another of basil, or one of chives, mint and parsley
2 oz (50 g) grated Parmesan cheese
salt and pepper

Have the pasta drained and kept warm. Beat the eggs fiercely with a tablespoon of water, as if you are making scrambled eggs. Heat the butter in a pan, pour in the eggs and add the herbs. Beat the mixture with a fork until the eggs are nearly done, then pour them over the pasta and toss all together thoroughly. Add the Parmesan and serve at once.

SPAGHETTI NEAPOLITAN

This is for garlic addicts only, but is also proof that the simplest ways with pasta are quite often the most satisfying. A writer who was living in Sicily introduced me to this way of eating spaghetti twenty years ago.

Slice as many cloves of garlic as you wish. After cooking the spaghetti, drain it well, add 2 tablespoons of olive oil and the sliced garlic, toss all for a moment over a gentle heat and serve at once. Sybarites may well add butter and black pepper to this at the table.

SPAGHETTI WITH TOMATO SAUCE 1

It is worth making this with fresh tomatoes, because the flavour is a world away from that of tinned tomatoes.

Heat a tablespoon of olive oil in a pan and add 5 sliced cloves of garlic; let them simmer for a moment to release their oil. Slice 10 tomatoes into small pieces, add them to the garlic and olive oil and keep them moving in the pan for about 3 minutes. They should be barely cooked. Add a tablespoon of chopped basil and seasoning, stir again, then pour the sauce over the cooked, drained spaghetti and serve it at once.

SPAGHETTI WITH TOMATO SAUCE 2

As good home-grown tomatoes are in season for only a short time, here is the recipe using tinned tomatoes.

¼ pt (150 ml) vegetable stock
6 bay leaves
a *bouquet garni*
1 glass red wine
1 14-oz (397-g) tin of tomatoes
6 crushed cloves of garlic
1 small tin of tomato *purée*
salt and pepper

Boil the stock with the bay leaves and the *bouquet garni* until reduced by half. Add the red wine and boil it again, until reduced by a third. Throw away the bay leaves and the *bouquet garni*. Place the tomatoes in the blender and pulp them. Add this, the garlic and the tomato *purée* to the stock and cook it until it begins to thicken.

SPAGHETTI WITH PESTO

The recipe for *Pesto*, my variation on the Genovese sauce made from basil and garlic, is on page 29. Cook and drain the spaghetti, and place it into an oiled and heated dish. Pour over several tablespoons of the cold *Pesto* and several knobs of butter. Toss the spaghetti well and serve it at once. Grated Parmesan may be served at the table.

BAKED RIGATONI WITH CREAM CHEESE

10 oz (275 g) *rigatoni*
6 oz (175 g) mixed cream cheese and curd cheese
2 oz (50 g) chopped walnuts
2 cloves of garlic (optional)
½ pt (300 ml) tomato sauce from *Spaghetti with Tomato Sauce 2*
½ pt (300 ml) water

Mix the two cheeses well together with the walnuts and the garlic if you are using it. Take a piece of *rigatoni* and scoop up the cheese so that the pasta has a filling. Place the filled *rigatoni* into a buttered casserole with a tight-fitting lid. To the tomato sauce, add ½ pt (300 ml) of water; heat the sauce, pour it over the *rigatoni* and bake it in a hot oven for 45 minutes.

PASTA WITH CREAM CHEESE

This is a simple but very good way with many varieties of pasta – spaghetti, macaroni, *tagliatelle*, *fettucine* or *rigatoni*.

10 oz (275 g) pasta
6 oz (175 g) cream cheese and curd cheese mixed
2 oz (50 g) Parmesan cheese
1 oz (25 g) softened butter
nutmeg
salt and pepper

Blend the three cheeses well into each other, adding the butter, nutmeg and seasoning. When the pasta is cooked and drained, put it into a buttered hot dish and stir the cheese mixture into it. Leave it in a warm oven for a few minutes until the cheese has just melted.

GNOCCHI VERDI

Most of us assume that *gnocchi* are made from either potatoes or semolina. This and the following recipe use neither, and both types or a mixture of both can be used in the third recipe.

1 lb (450 g) spinach
6 oz (175 g) cream cheese
2 oz (50 g) Parmesan cheese
butter
4 oz (100 g) flour
3 eggs
salt and pepper

After washing the spinach, squeeze as much of the water as you can out of it with your hands, then chop the leaves small, place them in a pan with a little butter, and cook them over a gentle heat, stirring the spinach and pressing it into the butter so that it is sealed. This should take no longer than 3 minutes. The stirring and sealing should not have allowed any moisture to escape from the leaves, but if there is some, drain it off now and leave the spinach to cool.

Mix the flour with the eggs and seasoning in a bowl until it has become a paste; add the cream cheese and the Parmesan, and mix it again. Finally, add the chopped spinach and make certain that it is mixed thoroughly. Cover the bowl and leave it overnight in the refrigerator.

Take the largest saucepan you possess and fill it with salted water. Bring the water to a simmer. Sprinkle the pastry board with flour and take out walnut-sized pieces of the *gnocchi* mixture. Roll them in flour and then drop them into the simmering water. (If the water boils too fiercely, the *gnocchi* will disintegrate.) When they rise to the surface, after 5–8 minutes, they are done. Take them out with a perforated spoon and let them drain in a colander.

Have a warm fireproof dish ready with a little more grated

Parmesan and melted butter in it, and slide the *gnocchi* into this. Keep the finished ones warm in the oven while the rest are being cooked.

1 **Cream Cheese Gnocchi**
  2 chopped green peppers
  2 chopped onions
  2 oz (50 g) butter
  4 oz (100 g) flour
  3 eggs
  ½ lb (225 g) cream cheese
  3 oz (75 g) Parmesan cheese
  salt and pepper
  nutmeg

Let the pepper and the onions soften in the butter over a gentle heat for about 10 minutes.

Mix the flour, eggs, two cheeses, seasoning and nutmeg well together, then add the peppers and onions. Leave overnight. The next day, cook the *gnocchi* as for the above recipe.

GNOCCHI IN PUFF PASTRY

Use the *Gnocchi Verdi* or the *Cream Cheese Gnocchi*. Roll the puff pastry thinly, then cut out small circles about the size of a tea saucer. Place a few *gnocchi* in each, so that the pastry casing is plump but will not burst open while cooking. It is a process of trial and error, and only experience tells you how much is correct. Sprinkle the *gnocchi* with Parmesan and put 2 teaspoons of sour cream in each case. Close the pastry cases by pinching the sides together. Brush the tops with beaten egg, place them on an oiled baking tray and cook them in a 400°F/200°C/Gas Mark 6 oven until the pastry is dark gold – about 20 minutes. Before serving, sprinkle each one with some chopped parsley.

FRENCH GNOCCHI

These use *pâte à choux*, which the British seem to associate only with *profiterolles*. The same cream puff pastry is used, omitting the sugar. They are neither difficult nor troublesome to make, and they open up a large range of savoury dishes. If mashed potato or cooked semolina is beaten into the paste, they become *gnocchi*; without that addition, they are called *quenelles*.

4 oz (100 g) flour
½ pt (300 ml) water
3 oz (75 g) butter
1 tsp salt
½ tsp black pepper
½ tsp nutmeg
4 eggs
1 lb (450 g) mashed potatoes
3 oz (75 g) Parmesan, Sage Derby or Double Gloucester cheese

Boil the water in a heavy thick-bottomed saucepan. In it melt the butter with the seasoning and nutmeg, then pour in the flour. Immediately take the saucepan from the heat and beat the mixture fiercely with a wooden spoon to amalgamate the flour and water mixture. Then place it back over a moderate heat and continue beating and stirring vigorously until the mixture congeals enough to leave the sides of the saucepan and to smear the bottom.

Remove the mixture from the heat, indent the centre with the spoon and drop in the first egg. Beat the pastry until the egg is quite absorbed. Continue with each of the eggs until the pastry is quite smooth. This is the basic *pâte à choux*.

To make this into the *gnocchi*, first stir the mashed potatoes over a gentle heat to get rid of any moisture. Add the cheese to the warm potatoes, then beat in the *pâte à choux*.

Take spoonfuls of the mixture and roll it on a floured board, making as many as you need. Any extra mixture will keep in the refrigerator if covered.

Bring salted water to a simmer in a large frying pan; slip the *gnocchi* into the water and poach them for 15 minutes. Don't let the water boil. The *gnocchi* should double their size and begin to roll over in the water. Drain them and serve with any of the following sauces or with *Leek Purée* (see page 22), fresh tomatoes, sliced mushrooms *sautéed* in butter, some of the *purées* on pages 37-8, or some of the sauces for *oeufs mollets* on pages 74-5.

At this stage the *gnocchi* can be put into a buttered fireproof dish, covered with the sauce and left for a few hours, until you need to reheat and serve them.

1 **Gnocchi Baked with Cheese**
Cover the *gnocchi* with a mixture of ¼ lb (100 g) of grated Double Gloucester and Parmesan cheeses. Place the dish in a hot oven for 10 minutes to warm, then under the grill to brown.

2 **Potato-herb Gnocchi**
Finely chop a handful of parsley, basil, chives or mint and beat them into the mixture before poaching the *gnocchi*. They then need nothing but melted butter poured over them.

3 **Potato and Onion Gnocchi**
Slice 3 large onions and *sauté* them in butter until soft. Place them in the blender and *purée* them. Pour this sauce over the *gnocchi* and brown them beneath the grill.

4 **Potato Gnocchi with Garlic Cream**
Skim 4 tablespoons of *Garlic Cream* from the bottled *Garlic Soup* (see page 29). Heat it and pour it over the *gnocchi*. This is a dish of such delicacy that the thought of it makes one's salivary glands work overtime.

QUENELLES

Make a *pâte à choux* and keep it warm. Have the oven heated to 425°F/220°C/Gas Mark 7. Butter a large baking sheet or tin. A French cook would shape the *quenelles* with a forcing bag, but I use a spoon. Take mounds of the *pâte à choux* with a dessert spoon and drop them on to the baking sheet, allowing 2 inches between each. They should be about 2 inches in diameter, and about 1 inch high. Using a spoon, one often gets mountain peaks, but these can be flattened with a brush dipped in beaten egg. Bake the *quenelles* for 20 minutes (when they will have doubled in size), then reduce the heat to 375°F/190°C/Gas Mark 5 and bake them for a further 10 minutes or until the puffs are golden brown and firm on the outside.

Remove them from the oven and slice off their tops. It is important to either do this at once or to make 1-inch slits in their sides. Otherwise they become soggy as they cool from the moisture of the centre. Turn off the oven and replace the puffs in it, leaving the door open, for 10 minutes. In this time you can finish making the sauces you will use.

1 **Fondue au Gruyère**
   1 oz (25 g) butter
   1 oz (25 g) flour
   ½ pt (300 ml) single cream
   salt and pepper
   1 egg yolk
   6 oz (175 g) grated Parmesan cheese
   2 oz (50 g) grated Gruyère cheese

Make a *roux* with the flour and the butter, ensuring that the flour is cooked thoroughly; it should take about 2 minutes over a gentle heat. Heat the cream with the seasoning, then add it to the *roux* away from the heat. The sauce will become very thick as you place it back over the heat and stir it vigorously for 1 minute.

Take it away from the heat again and beat in the egg yolk and the cheeses. It will then be very glutinous. Fill the *quenelles* with it, put their tops back on and serve them immediately.

2 **Onion, Garlic and Wine Sauce for Quenelles**
   3 sliced onions
   10 crushed cloves of garlic
   1 oz (25 g) butter
   1 glass dry white wine

Cook the onions and garlic in the butter until they are soft – about 5 minutes. Add the wine and let it boil until the sauce begins to reduce. Leave it to cool. Blend it to a *purée*, then reheat. Fill the *quenelles* with it and serve.

3 **Cold Quenelles with Green Peppercorn Sauce**
   This makes a superb supper dish for a hot summer. Make the *quenelles* about an hour before you need them. They don't react well to refrigeration, because they get tacky.

When they are cool, fill each one with the *Green Peppercorn Sauce* on page 75. The *Cold Dill Sauce* on the same page is also delicious.

POACHED HERB QUENELLES

Make a basic *pâte à choux* and, when it is still warm, beat in a handful of finely chopped fresh parsley, basil or mint. Take 2 wet dessert spoons; with one take some of the mixture, shape it with the other, then juggle it once or twice from one spoon to the other, so that you achieve a small cylinder. These can be rolled in flour like the *gnocchi*, but they will be lighter using this method.

Poach them in a pan of simmering salted water or, better still, in clear vegetable stock. They will take about 15 minutes. Remove them with a perforated spoon and drain them before placing them in a buttered fireproof dish. Sprinkle them with grated Parmesan and place them under a hot grill for a moment. Instead of the Parmesan, they can be served with either of the two following sauces.

1 **Cucumber and Cream Sauce**
Scoop out the seeds from a cucumber, then slice the flesh into 6 pieces lengthways, and across into 1-inch chunks. Sprinkle these with salt in a colander and leave them for an hour so that excess water will be lost. Wash the pieces well under the cold tap and pat them dry with a clean cloth. *Sauté* the cucumber pieces in 1 oz (25 g) of butter for about 10 minutes, so that they are softened but not brown. Add seasoning and ½ pint (300 ml) of single cream. Bring them to the boil, take them away from the heat, add an egg yolk and stir. Pour the sauce over the *Poached Herb Quenelles* and place them under a hot grill for a moment.

2 **Creamed Garlic Sauce**
¼ pt (150 ml) *Garlic Cream* (see page 29)
¼ pt (150 ml) single cream
pinch of cayenne pepper
salt
1 egg yolk

Heat the *Garlic Cream* with the single cream in a saucepan and add the seasoning. Take it from the heat and beat in the egg yolk.

SPICED POACHED QUENELLES

Make a *pâte à choux* (see page 143) and when it is still in the pan and warm, beat in a teaspoon of ground sesame and cumin seeds, a teaspoon of caraway and fennel seeds, a teaspoon of ground rosemary and one of salt, with a pinch of thyme and some hefty grinds of black pepper.

Poach these *quenelles* as for the *Poached Herb Quenelles* on page 147. A sauce made from fresh tomatoes is delicious with these, because the tangy spiced flavour of the *quenelles* needs the freshness. Thus, the cool *Cucumber and Yoghurt Sauce* on page 26 is also highly suitable.

Potato

I begin this group of recipes by giving seven of the greatest French classic dishes. However, as with all famous recipes, every cook differs as to the exact ingredients. Even the best cookbooks disagree, so what is right, within limits, is very much a matter of preference and of what experience has told you.

GRATIN DAUPHINOIS

No garlic, no cheese, no milk, no eggs. This is simple, classical and one of the best dishes in the world.

2 lb (1 kg) potatoes
1 oz (25 g) butter
1½ pt (900 ml) single cream
1 tsp nutmeg
salt and pepper

Peel the potatoes, then slice them on a *mandoline*, so that they are almost transparent. If you have no *mandoline* then you will have to slice them with a sharp knife – a longer process, but a perfectly satisfactory one.

Soak the sliced potatoes in cold water for 15 minutes, so they lose some of their starch. Drain them and pat them dry.

Use the butter to smear the inside of a *tian*. A shallow fireproof dish is necessary. I tried once to cook them in a *soufflé* dish, and the interior of the mixture was still slightly raw when the outside was ready.

Place a layer of the potatoes into the dish, season it with salt and pepper, add a bit of the nutmeg, then begin the next layer and continue as you began, seasoning as you go. There should be four or five layers, but no more. Pour the cream over the dish and leave it for a few minutes so the cream sinks down into the layers.

Place the dish into a preheated 300°F/150°C/Gas Mark 2 oven and let them cook slowly for 2½ hours.

I find the slow method of cooking allows the potatoes to soak up the cream and to become quite tender. At a stronger heat, the cream can curdle.

GRATIN LYONNAISE

2 lb (1 kg) potatoes
1 lb (450 g) sliced onions
2 oz (50 g) butter
salt and pepper
1 pt (600 ml) single cream

Peel and slice the potatoes very thinly, using a *mandoline* or a very sharp knife. Soak them as for the *Gratin Dauphinois*. Slice the onions and cook them in the butter until they are softened.

Butter the *tian* and place one layer of potatoes in the bottom. Spoon some of the onions over them and season them with salt and pepper. Continue until all the potatoes and onions are finished, ending with a potato layer and seasoning as you go. Pour the cream over the vegetables. You do not need as much cream here as for the *Gratin Dauphinois*, as the butter and the juice from the onions help to moisten the dish. Cook them in a 300°F/150°C/Gas Mark 2 oven for 2 hours.

GRATIN SAVOYARD

2 lb (1 kg) potatoes
3 oz (75 g) butter
4 oz (100 g) Double Gloucester cheese
salt and pepper
½ pt (300 ml) clear vegetable stock

Peel and slice the potatoes thinly, then soak them as for the *Gratin Dauphinois* on page 149. On each layer of potatoes place dabs of butter, sprinkle on some of the cheese and season with salt and pepper. Finish with a layer of potatoes, but reserve a good sprinkling of the cheese. Heat the vegetable stock and pour it over the potatoes. Top this with the remaining cheese. Cook this in a preheated oven at 425°F/220°C/Gas Mark 7, on the middle shelf. They should be cooked within half an hour. Test with a knife in the centre of the dish to see if the potatoes are soft throughout. If not, raise the heat and cook for another 10 minutes.

GRATIN PROVENÇALE

2 lb (1 kg) potatoes
1 lb (450 g) tomatoes
10 crushed cloves of garlic
1 lb (450 g) sliced onions
2 tbsp olive oil
salt and pepper
1 tbsp chopped basil

Peel, slice and soak the potatoes in the same manner as for *Gratin Dauphinois* on page 149. Peel the tomatoes after pouring boiling water over them to loosen the skins. Place them with the garlic in the blender and blend them to a liquid. Cook the onions in the olive oil until they are soft, then add the seasoning, the tomato and garlic liquid, and the basil.

Butter a *tian*, put a layer of sliced potatoes into it and spoon some of the mixture over them. Proceed in layers, seasoning each layer, and finish with the tomato-onion liquid.

Preheat the oven to 400°F/200°C/Gas Mark 6, cover the dish with foil and bake it for 30 minutes. Remove the foil and continue cooking it for another 15 minutes or until the top is well browned.

GRATIN ARDENNAISE

2 lb (1 kg) potatoes
1 tbsp juniper berries
1 pt (600 ml) milk
2 oz (50 g) butter
salt and pepper
2 oz (50 g) grated Parmesan cheese

Crush the juniper berries in a blender, a coffee grinder or with a mortar and pestle. Heat the milk. Slice the potatoes very thinly with a *mandoline* or a sharp knife, and prepare them for layering as for the *Gratin Dauphinois* on page 149. Butter a *tian* and spread a layer of the potatoes on the bottom. Dot it with dabs of butter, salt and pepper, and the juniper berries.

When all the potatoes and juniper berries are used up, pour the hot milk over the top and sprinkle the Parmesan over the top.

Cook it in the oven at a low heat for 2 hours.

GRATIN JURASSIEN

2 lb (1 kg) potatoes
½ lb (225 g) grated Gruyère cheese
2 oz (50 g) butter
salt and pepper
1 pt (600 ml) single cream

Peel, slice and prepare the potatoes as for the *Gratin Dauphinois* on page 149. Butter a *tian* or other shallow fireproof dish. Put a layer of potatoes on the dish, dot it with butter, season it and then sprinkle on some of the Gruyère cheese. Continue the layers until the potatoes, butter and cheese are used up. Pour the cream over the top and cook the dish in a slow oven for 2 hours. I fear that no other cheese will do; it is subtle in flavour and soft enough to merge with the potatoes and cream.

GRATIN DE CRÉCY

2 lb (1 kg) potatoes
1 lb (450 g) carrots
2 sliced onions
2 oz (50 g) butter
salt and pepper
1 pt (600 ml) single cream

Peel, slice and prepare the potatoes as for *Gratin Dauphinois* on page 149. Slice the carrots across and cook them with the onions in a little salted water for about 20 minutes, until the carrots are tender. Drain any excess liquor from them and reserve it for soup stock.

Butter a *tian* and in it put a layer of the potatoes. Place some of the carrot and onion mixture on top, dot this with butter, season it with salt and pepper, and continue these layers until the vegetables are used up. Finish with a layer of potatoes. Pour the cream over the top. Cook the dish in a slow oven for 2 hours.

POTATOES COOKED IN MILK

Peel 1 lb (450 g) of potatoes and cut them in slices about ¼ inch thick. Bring to the boil enough milk to cover the potatoes; season the milk liberally. Cook the potatoes in the milk until they are tender. It will take 30–45 minutes, for the milk must barely simmer or it will curdle and spoil the appearance of the dish. Drain them when cooked, reserving the milk, which will provide a stock for soup. Put the potatoes in a hot buttered dish and garnish them with chopped mint or parsley.

GOURMET PURÉE OF POTATOES

2 lb (1 kg) potatoes
½ pt (300 ml) single cream
2 oz (50 g) butter
10 oz (275 g) grated Gruyère
2 tbsp *Garlic Cream* (see page 29)
salt and pepper
pinch of nutmeg
chopped parsley

Boil the potatoes in their skins. Drain them and when they are cooked, peel them and mash them over a little heat to ensure that they are quite dry. Heat the remaining ingredients, except the parsley, in a thick-bottomed saucepan, stirring all the time. Before it boils, tip in the dry *purée* of potato and take it away from the heat as you stir it in. It should be very smooth. Place the saucepan back on to the heat until the mixture is hot, turn it out into a heated dish, sprinkle it with the parsley and serve at once.

If there is any *purée* left over, roll spoonfuls of it in flour and fry them in olive oil until golden. For use of this dish with poached eggs, see page 88.

POTATO CROQUETTES

Mash 1 lb (450 g) of boiled potatoes, add 1 oz (25 g) of butter and 4 oz (100 g) of grated Sage Derby cheese with 1 egg, salt, pepper and a pinch of nutmeg. Let it cool in the refrigerator for a few hours or overnight, as the mixture is always better to handle when cold.

Roll pieces of the mixture the size of a crab apple first in flour, then in beaten egg and finally in breadcrumbs, and fry them in a hot vegetable oil.

NEW POTATOES WITH CREAM SAUCE

Boil new potatoes in their skins until they are tender. Make the *Sauce à la Crème* on page 24. Drain the potatoes, tip them into a heated dish and pour the sauce over them. Garnish with a little chopped parsley.

POTATOES COOKED IN VEGETABLE STOCK

Scrub some large potatoes, cut them in quarters and lay them at the bottom of a large pan. Pour over the *Brown Vegetable Stock* on page 45. Let them simmer until they have absorbed all the flavour and most of the liquid – about 30 minutes. Turn them out into a fireproof dish, sprinkle with a little grated Parmesan and place under a hot grill for a moment.

POMMES DE TERRE SABLÉES

This is a delicious way to cook new potatoes when they are very small. Scrub them, then melt about 3 oz (75 g) of butter in a thick-bottomed pan and put the small potatoes into it so that they fit tightly at the bottom. Cook them over a gentle heat, as the butter must not burn, and turn them over so that they brown on all their surfaces. When they are cooked, in about 25 minutes, sprinkle a couple of tablespoons of bread-crumbs into the butter and shake the pan. The breadcrumbs will turn crisp in a few moments.

BAKED POTATOES IN STOCK AND WHITE WINE

Scrub the skins of some large potatoes, cut them into quarters, then lay them in a casserole dish. Have the oven preheated to a medium heat, dab 2 oz (50 g) of butter over the potatoes, then add enough hot *White Vegetable Stock* (see page 45) to cover them. Pour in a glass of dry white wine and season well. Put the lid on the casserole and cook in the oven at 375°F/190°C/Gas Mark 5 for 1 hour.

Take them from the oven and pour off the sauce into a mixing bowl that has 2 egg yolks in it; stir together well so that the sauce thickens. Sprinkle the potatoes with a handful of chopped parsley and chives, then pour over the sauce and replace the dish in the oven for a few moments.

POTATOES COOKED IN A BAG

The roasting bags that you can now buy are perfect for this dish. Choose good new potatoes, wash and dry them, then put them into the bag with 3 oz (75 g) of butter, salt, pepper and several sprigs of mint. Shake the bag well. Tie it and place it in a medium oven for 1 hour.

POTATOES WITH TOMATOES AND BLACK OLIVES

1 lb (450 g) potatoes
½ lb (225 g) tomatoes
3 tbsp olive oil
salt and pepper
3 bay leaves
1 tbsp tomato *purée*
12 stoned black olives
2 tbsp breadcrumbs

Peel the potatoes and slice them into ¼-inch rounds. Peel the tomatoes and slice them; put them into a saucepan with the olive oil, salt, pepper and bay leaves. Cook this for a moment, then stir in the tomato *purée*. Add ¼ pint (150 ml) of boiling water.

Butter a *tian* or shallow fireproof dish, place the potatoes and the olives into this and then pour the tomato sauce over it. Cover with foil. Cook in a medium oven for 1 hour, then test whether the potatoes are cooked through. When they are tender, sprinkle the breadcrumbs over the top and place it under a hot grill to brown the crumbs.

POTATOES IN GARLIC STOCK

Peel 1 lb (450 g) of old potatoes and slice them into ½-inch chunks. Choose a thick-bottomed saucepan, throw the potatoes into it and add 1 oz (25 g) of butter; season well. Let them simmer for 1 hour in enough clear garlic stock from under the *Garlic Cream* (see page 51) to cover the potatoes. There should be little stock left by that time. Drain whatever there is into a mixing bowl with an egg yolk in it, stirring the yolk into the stock. Turn the potatoes out into a dish and pour the sauce over them. Sprinkle the top with a little chopped parsley or mint.

SAUTÉED POTATOES WITH ONIONS

Boil 1 lb (450 g) of potatoes in their skins for 10 minutes; drain them and, when cool, peel them. Slice them into $\frac{1}{4}$-inch rounds. Meanwhile, slice 1 lb (450 g) of onions and *sauté* them in a frying pan in a tablespoon of olive oil. When the onions are soft, throw in the potatoes. Raise the heat and cook them for a further 10 minutes, turning the potatoes and onions over so that they brown together.

Turn them out into a fireproof dish and place them un-covered in a hot oven for a further 15 minutes. Both the potatoes and the onions should be crisp and brown.

PURÉE OF POTATOES WITH CREAM CHEESE

1 lb (450 g) potatoes
6 oz (175 g) cream cheese
1 oz (25 g) butter
salt and pepper
pinch of nutmeg
2 oz (50 g) grated Parmesan cheese

Peel the potatoes and boil them until tender; drain them well and mash them with the butter and the salt and pepper. Then place them back over the heat and stir, adding the nutmeg and the cream cheese, stirring the latter in a spoonful at a time. When it has melted and amalgamated with the *purée*, turn out on to a buttered fireproof dish, sprinkle with the Parmesan and place under a hot grill for a few moments.

GRATED POTATO PANCAKES

2 lb (1 kg) large potatoes
6 oz (175 g) cream cheese
6 oz (175 g) grated Sage Derby cheese
2 oz (50 g) flour
salt and pepper
2 eggs
1 finely chopped onion
handful of chopped parsley
¼ pt (150 ml) single cream
olive oil and butter for frying

Peel the potatoes and grate them. Let them soak for half an hour in a bowl of water, then drain them and squeeze them dry in a cloth.

Mash the cream cheese with the flour in a bowl and add the salt, pepper, eggs, Sage Derby, onion and parsley. Mix well, then add the cream. Finally, stir in the potatoes.

Have a frying pan with a mixture of oil and butter in it. Heat it so the butter foams, then with a ladle drop some of the mixture into the pan, in cakes about 2½ inches in diameter (if they are too wide they are liable to break). Cook these four at a time, allowing them to get golden brown before turning them over and doing the other side. Keep the first lot warm in the oven while you do the rest.

They can be made beforehand and heated in the oven for 10 minutes before serving. As with everything else though, they are better eaten immediately.

BAKED SPICED POTATOES

4 large potatoes
½ pt (300 ml) yoghurt
5 crushed bay leaves
1 tsp each turmeric powder, *garam masala* and chilli powder
2 tbsp oil
½ tsp brown sugar
5 crushed cloves of garlic
salt and pepper
handful of chopped coriander leaves

Fry the bay leaves and the other spices in the oil for a few moments, then stir in the sugar and the garlic. Add the salt and pepper and mix the spiced mixture with the yoghurt.

Peel the potatoes and boil them whole for about 12 minutes. Drain them. Prick them all over with a fork and then roll them in the yoghurt paste, making sure they are covered in it. It is best to pour the paste into a large fireproof shallow dish and to roll each potato around in it. Put the dish into a preheated oven at 400°F/200°C/Gas Mark 6 for about 30 minutes, and sprinkle it with the coriander leaves before serving.

POTATO CURRY WITH YOGHURT

Peel and slice 1 lb (450 g) of old potatoes, cut them into ¼-inch slices, wash the starch from them and dry them in a cloth. Place them in the bottom of a large casserole dish and pour over enough of the *Curry Sauce* (see page 25) to cover them. For a hot curry, add the chillies. Put them into a preheated oven at 400°F/200°C/Gas Mark 6 for 30 minutes, then lower the heat to slow and leave them for a further 15 minutes.

Mix a handful of chopped coriander leaves with ½ pint (300 ml) of yoghurt and pour this over the curried potatoes; then brown them under a hot grill.

POTATO, GINGER AND ONION TARKARI

Tarkaris are Indian vegetable dishes where the vegetables are fried in ghee (clarified butter) and their own juices and where, by sudden intense heat at the conclusion of cooking, the spices impregnate the vegetables.

However, in most Indian recipes, some of the vegetables are partly-cooked beforehand. This seems to me a waste. By slicing the vegetables in the Chinese manner – diagonally or thinly on the *mandoline* – one can avoid this step.

Peel 3 large potatoes and slice them on the *mandoline* or cut them thinly. Rinse them beneath a cold tap and dry them in a cloth. Slice 2 large onions and about 2 oz (50 g) of ginger root, and heat 2 tablespoons of vegetable oil in a frying pan. Throw in the potatoes, onion and ginger. Cover the pan and leave it for about 20 minutes over a gentle heat. Then add 2 chopped green chillies and ⅓ teaspoon of paprika, turmeric and cumin seeds. Season it well, then uncover the pan. Raise the heat, stirring and shaking the pan to avoid burning the vegetables in the final cooking which should take about 4 minutes. The potatoes and onions should become crisp. Serve them with a sprinkling of chopped coriander leaves.

BAKED POTATOES

These are simple to cook and delicious to eat just with butter. Nearly all of us enjoy them, and I've never known a child who did not express delight when presented with one.

Any potato, new or old, of whatever size, can be baked successfully. The older potato will have a thicker and crustier skin – that is all. Scrub the skins, prick them with a fork (or else the potato may burst while cooking) and place the potatoes in a medium oven on the top rack. A potato 3 inches long by 2 inches wide would take roughly an hour, but how large or small the potato is regulates the amount of cooking time.

Parsley or garlic butters, sour cream with chives or mint can all be used to spread on the hot potato instead of plain butter. *Aïoli* (see page 215) is also delicious. Yet the best is the simplest, derived from my exasperation that a bunch of mint added to new potatoes when the potatoes are boiled, never gives enough taste of mint – all the flavour is lost in the water. Hence, mint butter with baked potatoes.

6 oz (175 g) chopped mint
6 oz (175 g) softened butter

Chop the mint finely as soon as you have picked it. Let the butter soften at room temperature, then mix both together and refrigerate.

The potatoes can also be stuffed in various ways, the most common methods being the following ones.

1 **Baked Potato Soufflé**
Always choose the largest possible potatoes for stuffing. When they are baked, cut them in half, scoop out half of the flesh and keep it for soups or other dishes. Scoop out the rest of the flesh of 4 potatoes and mash it well with 2 egg yolks, ¼ lb (100 g) of grated Double Gloucester cheese and

2 oz (50 g) grated Parmesan. Beat the 2 egg whites until they are stiff and fold them into the potato mixture. Half-fill each potato shell with the mixture and place them back into a hot oven for about 15 minutes, so that the fillings will rise and brown.

2 **Baked Potatoes with Garlic Cream**
Bake the potatoes, then slit them, scoop out the flesh and reserve half of it for other dishes. Beat the rest of the potato flesh to a *purée* and add enough *Garlic Cream* (see page 29) to make a smooth paste. Place the skins with the mixture inside them under a hot grill until the surface bubbles and begins to brown.

3 **Baked Potatoes Stuffed with Parsnip and Caraway**
Bake, split and hollow out 4 potatoes. Add to the potato flesh an equal quantity of mashed parsnip flavoured with caraway (see *Parsnip and Caraway Falafels* on page 204). Mix them well, pile them back into the shells and reheat them in the oven.

Parsnips were popular in England in the Middle Ages. It was one of the reasons why the Elizabethans accepted the potato, for it was the sweet variety that was introduced into England then.*

4 **Baked Potatoes Stuffed with Onion**
Bake, split and hollow out 4 potatoes, reserving half of the flesh for other dishes. Slice 3 onions and *sauté* them in butter until they are soft. Season them well, then cool them and blend to a *purée*. Add this to the remaining half of the potato flesh and mix well. Fill each potato shell with the mixture, sprinkle with a little Parmesan and place the potatoes back in the oven for 10 minutes or until they are beginning to brown on top.

5 **Baked Potatoes Stuffed with Leeks**
Bake, split and hollow out some potatoes. Mix the flesh with an equal quantity of the *Leek Purée* on page 22.

---

* Caryl Brahms and S. J. Simon may have been confused when, in *No Bed for Bacon* (Michael Joseph), they invent the scene where Queen Elizabeth I spits out the potato complaining that there is not enough salt in it. She might well have asked for honey instead.

Sprinkle the tops with grated Parmesan and reheat the potatoes in the oven. If an egg is whipped into the mixture, you will then have a type of egg and potato tart in a potato shell.

For a variation on this, use *Spinach Purée* instead of the leek one.

POTATO SALAD

Make this salad always with new potatoes and do not skin them.

Boil 1 lb (450 g) of potatoes until tender. Have ready ¼ pint (150 ml) of *sauce vinaigrette* with 2 crushed cloves of garlic in it. Drain the potatoes and tip them into the *vinaigrette*; toss them well and let them cool in it.

Before serving, add a handful of chopped parsley, mint or chives (or a mixture of all three) with 3 tablespoons of mayonnaise. Toss the potatoes again so that they are all covered with the herbs and the mayonnaise.

CURRIED POTATO SALAD

Toss 1 lb (450 g) of hot, drained boiled potatoes in ¼ pint (150 ml) of *vinaigrette sauce* with 2 crushed cloves of garlic in it. Mix 1 tablespoon of the *Curry Sauce* on page 25 with 2 tablespoons of mayonnaise. When the potatoes are cool, toss them in this curried mayonnaise. Add chopped coriander leaves and serve.

CHAPTER VIII

Main Courses

In vegetarian cooking it is difficult to decide exactly whether a dish is an *entrée*, a luncheon dish, an *hors d'oeuvre* or even an appetizer, and equally if some would be considered as the main course or not. All depends on whether one is cooking for a large dinner party, when one would select many small dishes as well as one or two substantial ones, or merely for a modest supper for two. Therefore, this chapter continues with a number of dishes which are filling, although some may seem too much trouble to make for anything but a dinner party. In the second half of the chapter though, there are recipes which are less trouble and which one could call vegetable *entrées*.

STUFFED PANCAKES

Most cooks have discovered their own favourite batter and keep to those well-tried proportions of milk, water, flour and egg. But as in all the simplest cooking, there are many permutations. The lightest batter uses no milk and has the egg white whipped up and beaten into it. What all cooks would agree on is that the *crêpe* or pancake must never be leathery; such an effect is caused by too much flour and milk to only one egg. Yet, if you hasten in horror from that error and lavishly break eggs into the flour, you will achieve at the end something like a bad omelette. As in all matters, a balance must be sought and achieved. What batter you choose depends on how you will use the pancakes. When they are eaten hot and stuffed, as in this recipe, you will need a batter that is light but strong enough to take the filling without letting it seep. This recipe makes enough for 4 people.

batter :
4 oz (100 g) flour
2 eggs
½ pt (300 ml) milk and water mixed
½ tsp salt
1 oz (25 g) melted butter
filling :
4 thinly-sliced onions
2 hard-boiled eggs
1 tbsp wine vinegar
1 tsp dill seed
handful of chopped parsley
salt and pepper
1 carton sour cream
olive oil
. grated Parmesan cheese

For the batter, measure the flour and salt into a mixing bowl, make a well in the centre and break the eggs into it. With a wooden spoon mix the eggs into the flour to get a smooth paste. Add the melted butter and continue to stir, then add the water and milk. Use an egg whisk to beat the batter so that the flour paste is well mixed. Refrigerate the batter for an hour or two. Beat the batter again before making the pancakes. It should be thick enough to coat a spoon.

Alternatively, the batter can be made in the liquidizer where all the ingredients are popped in and it is blended at high speed for a moment or two. It is easier but you may get the stray lump of flour here and there.

Let the onions marinate for an hour in the wine vinegar, then strain them carefully and reserve the vinegar for a sauce. Crush the dill and shell, chop and mash the eggs. Add these and the parsley to the onion, mix well and season; then add the sour cream.

Put not more than a teaspoon of olive oil into a shallow pan and heat it so that the oil runs over the surface enough to make it shine. If there are any drops of oil, pour them off into a jug to use later – when and if the pan becomes too dry. Use a ladle for measuring the batter (about 4 dessertspoons) and, after pouring it into the pan, make sure it runs evenly over the bottom by moving and rocking the pan gently. Each *crêpe* will

take less than a minute to cook on both sides. Turn each one
out as it is ready on to greaseproof paper and continue until
the batter is finished.

Then fill each *crêpe* with some of the mixture. Roll them up,
place them in a buttered *tian* or shallow fireproof dish and
put them into a preheated 400°F/200°C/Gas Mark 6 oven,
after sprinkling the Parmesan over the top. Leave them for
10 minutes or until you see the centre heave a little with the
heat. Transfer them to a hot grill for a few moments to ensure
that the top is brown.

One can fill pancakes with many different mixtures. For
instance, they can be spread with *purées* made from pulses and
then rolled like a Swiss roll. This is earthy and filling, but if
you are generous with the spices and herbs it can be a revela-
tion. Other fillings can be used, and the following are but a
few suggestions.

1 **Stuffed Spinach Pancakes**
  1 recipe for *pancake batter*, made up (see page 163)
  1 lb (450 g) chopped raw spinach
  1 bunch sliced spring onions
  2 oz (50 g) butter
  salt and pepper
  6 oz (175 g) grated Sage Derby cheese
  White Sauce (see page 28)

Cook the spinach and the onions in the butter in a saucepan
for 5 minutes, until the spinach has reduced to a third of
its bulk. Chop it in the saucepan with the edge of a wooden
spoon, drain off any liquid, then add the seasoning and the
cheese. Stir until the cheese has begun to melt. Fill the
pancakes with this mixture, put them in a buttered fireproof dish and cover them with the *White Sauce*. Then
place them under a hot grill until they begin to bubble and
brown.

2 **Aubergine Pancakes**
  Make up the pancakes as for the *Stuffed Pancakes* on page
  163. Use any one of the aubergine *purées* on pages 42–3.
  Stuff the pancakes with it, hot, then put them in a buttered
  fireproof dish, cover them with the *Sauce Messine* (see
  page 27) and place the dish under a hot grill to brown.

3 **Cheese Pancakes with Sauce Moutarde**
   1 recipe of pancake batter, made up (see page 163)
   6 oz (175 g) cream cheese
   6 oz (175 g) grated Sage Derby cheese
   1 egg
   salt and pepper
   Sauce Moutarde (see page 23)

   Mash the two cheeses, the egg and the seasoning together
   in a bowl. Use this to fill the pancakes, then lay them in a
   buttered fireproof dish and pour the *Sauce Moutarde* over
   them. Place them in a hot oven for 5 minutes, then under
   the grill for another minute.

4 **Cheese and Mushroom Pancakes**
   1 recipe for pancake batter, made up (see page 163)
   6 oz (175 g) cream cheese
   ½ lb (225 g) sliced mushrooms
   1 bunch sliced spring onions
   salt and pepper
   1 egg
   butter
   Cheese Sauce or *Green Sauce* (see pages 28 and 26)

   Mix the cheese, seasoning and egg together. *Sauté* the
   mushrooms and the spring onions in a little butter for a
   couple of minutes, then stir in the cheese mixture; take it
   from the heat and beat it so that the ingredients blend.
   Fill the pancakes with the mixture, put them in a buttered
   shallow fireproof dish, pour over a thin *Cheese Sauce* or the
   Green Sauce, place the dish in a hot oven for 5 minutes and
   then transfer the dish to beneath the grill for a moment.

5 **Stuffed Pancakes Provençale**
   Prepare some pancakes, as on page 163. Cook together
   1 lb (450 g) of chopped, home-grown tomatoes and 6
   crushed cloves of garlic in a tablespoon of olive oil for
   10 minutes, in a covered saucepan on a gentle heat. Take
   the pan from the heat, stir in a handful of chopped basil, and
   add enough breadcrumbs to soak up the juices. Taste and
   season; you may feel that it needs a teaspoon of tomato
   purée. Fill the pancakes, put them in a buttered fireproof

dish, sprinkle them liberally with grated Parmesan, then place them under a hot grill to brown.

6 **Pancakes Stuffed with Leeks**
Make up a batch of pancakes from the recipe on page 163. Slice both the green and the white parts of 1 lb (450 g) leeks, having first cleaned them, and *sauté* them in 1 dessertspoon of butter in a closed pan for 10 minutes. Allow them to cool, then blend them into a *purée*. Add ¼ pint (150 ml) of single cream and season it with salt and pepper.

Make a thin *roux* with 1 oz (25 g) of butter and 1 oz (25 g) of flour, and add the creamed leek *purée* to it. Heat the mixture until it begins to thicken, then fill the pancakes with it. Put them in a buttered fireproof dish, dot the tops of the pancakes with dabs of cream cheese and place them under a hot grill to brown.

7 **Avocado Pancakes**
Scoop the flesh from 3 avocados and add 2 crushed cloves of garlic to it. Mash it to a smooth paste with 2 tablespoons of double cream. Taste it and season, making sure that it is not too bland; it may need more black pepper or another clove of garlic. Make up a batch of pancakes from the recipe on page 163. Fill each pancake with this mixture, put them in a buttered fireproof dish and sprinkle grated Parmesan over the top. Place the dish under a hot grill for a minute or so, then serve.

SPICED PANCAKES

4 oz (100 g) flour
1 oz (25 g) home-made curry powder (see page 25)
1 egg
¼ pt (150 ml) water (or milk and water mixed)
pinch of salt

Mix all the ingredients together to make a batter. Fry a spoonful at a time on a hot oiled pan, then drain it on greaseproof paper. If the pancakes are small, spread them with sour cream, roll them up and serve them as appetizers. If you make them larger, stuff them with any of the fillings given for the *Stuffed Pancakes* on pages 164–6.

TIMBALE DE CRÊPES

Have ready a large buttered *soufflé* dish; make about 20 pan-cakes (treble amounts on page 163) and cut 10 of them in half. Line the sides of the dish with the halves, with their lower points meeting in the centre of the bottom of the dish and the upper points lying over its rim.

Now fill the dish with layers of various stuffings, separating each one from the next with a pancake. If any are too big or of an irregular shape, trim them. Start, for example, with the spinach filling (see page 164). Add a pancake, then put in the cheese and mushroom filling on page 165; another pancake, then the leek or the tomato fillings on pages 165–6, and so on. When the dish is almost full, fold in the ends of the pancakes outside the dish, and spread a final pancake over the top.

As with the *timbales* (see page 84), place the *soufflé* dish in a baking tin of boiling water, put it in the oven at 350°F/180°C/Gas Mark 4 and leave it for about 40 minutes. Have ready a buttered warm serving dish. Take the *timbale* out of the oven, leave it to settle for a few moments, then put the warmed dish over it and invert the *timbale* out of the *soufflé* dish and on to the serving dish. Cut the *timbale* like a cake and serve it with a sauce that will go well with the fillings you have chosen.

You can make this dish with the *Spiced Pancakes* (see page 166) and serve it with *Sweet-and-sour Sauce* (see page 26).

STUFFED CABBAGE

Use a Savoy cabbage and blanch it whole by plunging it into boiling salted water and leaving it there for 3 minutes. Take it out, let it drain, place it upon a wooden board and carefully unfold each leaf. It will open like a grandiloquent flower.

You can now either extract the heart of the cabbage, cutting it out with a sharp grapefruit knife and adding it, chopped, to whatever filling you choose, or you can leave the heart as it is. It depends on how much filling you have.

Spread the filling on each leaf, starting from the centre and working outwards. Then tie the cabbage back into its original shape, place it in a covered casserole with 1 pint (600 ml) of stock and then cook it slowly for 3 hours in a slow oven.

1 **Chou Farci Provençale**
Tinned tomatoes can be used here, because the long cooking would destroy the fresh flavour that the home-grown tomatoes have.

1 blanched and drained Savoy cabbage (see *Stuffed Cabbage*, above)
1 large tin of tomatoes
crushed cloves from 1 head of garlic
1 tsp crushed caraway seeds
1 tbsp olive oil
2 oz (50 g) grated Gruyère cheese
handful of chopped fresh basil or parsley
2 eggs
about 6 oz (175 g) breadcrumbs
tomato *purée* (optional)
salt and pepper
4 cloves
1 pt (600 ml) *Brown Vegetable Stock* (see page 45)

Peel and crush the garlic cloves and cook them, with the caraway seeds, for a few minutes in the olive oil over a gentle heat. Drain the tomatoes, then blend them; add the resulting liquid to the garlic mixture. Let it simmer for 10 minutes, add the Gruyère and stir until it has melted.

Take the pan away from the heat and add the herbs; then beat in the eggs. It will be very liquid. Add the bread-crumbs until it has become a paste. You may need more than the suggested amount. Taste it and see whether you want to add any tomato *purée*; season it.

Spread the leaves of the cabbage with this mixture. Close and tie the cabbage, and stick the cloves in the top. Heat the stock, pour it over the cabbage in the casserole and cook it slowly for 3 hours.

2 **Stuffed Cabbage with Walnuts**
1 blanched and drained Savoy cabbage (see page 167)
¼ lb (100 g) dried chestnuts
½ lb (225 g) chopped walnuts
1 tbsp crushed black peppercorns
1 tbsp olive oil
6 crushed cloves of garlic

salt
2 eggs
2 oz (50 g) uncooked rice
4 oz (100 g) breadcrumbs
1 pt (600 ml) *Brown Vegetable Stock* (see page 45)

Pour boiling water over the chestnuts and leave them for
an hour; then boil them for 45 minutes. Drain them and
chop them up coarsely. Cook the peppercorns in the olive
oil, add the chestnuts, garlic, walnuts and salt, and simmer
for a few minutes.

Take the mixture away from the heat, cool it, then beat
in the eggs. Add the rice and breadcrumbs until you
achieve a workable paste. Proceed as for the *Stuffed
Cabbage* (see page 168).

3 **Stuffed Cabbage with Onions and Aïllade Sauce**
   1 blanched and drained Savoy cabbage (see page 167)
   1 lb (450 g) sliced onions
   4 tbsp *Aïllade* (see page 29)
   2 oz (50 g) butter
   2 eggs
   6 oz (175 g) breadcrumbs
   salt and pepper

Melt the butter in a pan and *sauté* the onions in it until they
are soft. When cool, blend them to a *purée*. Beat in the eggs,
and *Aïllade*, the breadcrumbs and the seasoning to make a
paste. Proceed as for the *Stuffed Cabbage* on page 168.

4 **Stuffed Cabbage with Mushrooms and Peppers**
   1 blanched and drained Savoy cabbage (see page 167)
   4 sliced green peppers
   ½ lb (225 g) mushrooms
   1 sliced onion
   1 tbsp olive oil
   2 eggs
   1 tsp each crushed cumin or coriander
   pinch of mace
   6 oz (175 g) breadcrumbs
   salt and pepper
   1 pt (600 ml) *Brown Vegetable Stock* (see page 45)

Cook the peppers, mushrooms and onion in the olive oil until they are soft. When cool, beat in the eggs, spices, breadcrumbs and seasoning. Stuff the cabbage as for the *Stuffed Cabbage* on page 168.

STUFFED PEPPERS 1

This and the next recipe are alternatives to the more common filling which uses a flavoured rice. This one uses fresh herbs with spices and cheese, and is as good cold as it is hot.

6 small green or red sweet peppers
¼ lb (100 g) mushrooms
3 sliced onions
olive oil
2 oz (50 g) celery leaves
2 oz (50 g) parsley
2 large grated carrots
3 crushed cloves of garlic
1 lemon
1 tsp chopped dill
¼ lb (100 g) grated Cheddar cheese
salt and pepper

Cut the tops off the peppers, remove the stalks, seeds and pith, and put the tops aside. Gently fry the mushrooms and the onions in the olive oil until they are soft and have released their liquids. Chop the celery leaves and the parsley and mix them with the carrots in a bowl. Add the mushrooms and the onions to the carrot mixture, with the remaining oil and vegetable liquids, the garlic, lemon zest, dill, cheese and seasoning. Mix well together.

Stuff the peppers with the filling, place them in the saucepan and put their tops back on. Squeeze the juice of the lemon over them and pour in enough water to surround them half-way up their sides. Let them simmer gently for 45 minutes, when they can be picked out with a perforated spoon and left to drain for a moment before serving. The liquid that is left makes a good basic stock for soups.

STUFFED PEPPERS 2

Use green peppers for this recipe. Slice diagonally a variety of root vegetables: parsnips, carrots, turnips and potatoes. Partly-cook them in the *Hot Marinade* (see page 115). Heat a tablespoon of cooking oil and add to it 1 teaspoon each of coriander, *garam masala*, turmeric and paprika. Add also a grated ginger root and, depending on how hot you want the dish to be, some chopped green chillies. Cook them gently for a few minutes.

Drain the root vegetables from the marinade, add to them the juice from a lemon and the fried spices. Mix all together well in a bowl and fill each pepper with the mixture.

Fit the peppers snugly together at the bottom of a casserole or a *marmite* and pour into the dish 1 pint (600 ml) of *Brown Vegetable Stock* (see page 45). Cook it in a preheated oven at a medium heat for 45 minutes.

STUFFED PEPPERS 3

6 peppers
1 14-oz (397-g) tin of tomatoes
2 chopped onions
crushed cloves from 1 head of garlic
1 tbsp olive oil
1 tsp dried basil
6 oz (175 g) uncooked rice
salt and pepper
1 pt (600 ml) *Brown Vegetable Stock* (see page 45)

Drain the tomatoes and *purée* them in the blender. Cook the onion and the garlic in the olive oil over a gentle heat until they are soft, then add the tomatoes and the basil. Simmer for 10 minutes.

Take the sauce off the heat and stir in the uncooked rice. Season it and half-fill each pepper with the mixture, leaving room for the rice to expand in the cooking. Fit the peppers into a casserole and pour the stock over them. Cook them for 45 minutes in a medium oven.

DOLMADES (Stuffed Vine Leaves)

All Greek shops sell packets of vine leaves which are soaked in brine. You need to place them in a bowl, scald them and allow the leaves to float and to disentangle themselves from one another. Leave them to soak while you make the filling, but be careful to rinse the leaves in a colander beneath cold water before using them. The vine leaves have a characteristic flavour and colour, but each country of the Middle East varies its herbs, spices and other filling ingredients. There is no definitive version of *dolmades*, as with all popular dishes. Therefore, the following recipe can be the source of your own experiments.

½ lb (225 g) drained vine leaves
½ lb (225 g) uncooked rice
2 finely chopped onions
2 tbsp finely chopped celery leaves
1 tsp each crushed dill, thyme and oregano
salt and pepper
¼ pt (150 ml) olive oil
juice of 2 lemons
4–5 crushed cloves of garlic

Scald the rice and leave it for a few moments in the boiling water; then rinse it under a cold tap. Add the onions, garlic, celery, herbs and seasoning.

Place a teaspoon of the mixture in the centre of a vine leaf (the larger leaves will need more, the smaller ones less). Roll the leaf over the filling, tucking in the sides as you go, like making hospital corners on a bed. Choose a thick-bottomed pan and lay any vegetables you have to hand, such as outside cabbage leaves, leek tops, onion skins etc on the bottom in a level layer. This gives you an excellent stock, but its main purpose is to cushion the *dolmades* so that they neither stick nor burn. Pack the stuffed vine leaves in so that they are wedged together in a layer. If you have more, add a second layer. If there are not enough to be wedged in tightly, use a slice of onion, carrot, pepper or garlic cloves to fill the gap, so that the *dolmades* do not unravel themselves.

Pour over the olive oil and the lemon juice with enough water to rise 2–3 inches above the top layer. Cook them slowly over a gentle heat, but watch that they never dry out. More water might have to be poured into the pan, but it is best to allow the *dolmades* to first soak up the oil and lemon water to enhance their flavour, instead of drowning them in water from the start. They will need from 1½–2 hours, depending on how gentle the heat is.

These are, of course, delicious cold too, served with a squeeze of lemon juice over them.

I prefer to bake them in the oven at a medium to low heat, when they can be ignored for 2½ hours, then taken out, left in the stock overnight and either reheated the following day or eaten cold. Some recipes advise adding soaked chick peas, crushed in a mortar, to the filling. This gives a less firm texture to the completed *dolmades*, as the chick peas provide a slight mush which tends to make them spongy. I like them firm and spicy.

STUFFED AUBERGINES 1

3 small aubergines
3 large sliced onions
1 14-oz (397-g) tin of tomatoes
1 tbsp sesame seeds
olive oil
5 crushed cloves of garlic
¼ lb (100 g) grated Parmesan, Gruyère or Double Gloucester cheese, according to taste
breadcrumbs

Slice the aubergines lengthways, pour the olive oil on the exposed centre, sprinkle them with the sesame seeds and bake them in a medium oven for 45 minutes. Then take them out and, when they are cool enough to handle, scoop out all the flesh from the centre and place it in a bowl, leaving the shells to be filled later. This cooking will have allowed the sesame seeds to release their flavour, for they are a spice that needs baking or cooking in some manner before being added to food.

Soften the onions in olive oil, drain the tomatoes and add them to the onions. Add the garlic to the aubergines with the cheese, then put both mixtures together. Fill the shells with this, sprinkle the breadcrumbs over the top, place the filled shells in a moderate oven to reheat, then put them under a hot grill to make the breadcrumbs crisp. Serve at once.

Both the zest from the lemon and its juice can be added to sharpen the flavours. This will feed six people; they are more filling than they seem.

STUFFED AUBERGINES 2

An alternative method of preparation is to slice the aubergines lengthways, allowing one-half for each person. Then, with a grapefruit knife, gouge out the flesh, leaving ⅛-inch of flesh on the peel.

3 small aubergines
2 chopped onions
½ lb (225 g) cooked Jerusalem artichokes
2 tbsp olive oil
4 tbsp *Aïllade* (see page 29)

Heat the olive oil in a pan and add the onions and the aubergine flesh. Cook until the vegetables are soft, then add the Jerusalem artichokes; stir the mixture and take it away from the flame. Fill the aubergine shells, then pour over enough *Aïllade* to cover the top surfaces. Bake them in a medium oven for 45 minutes.

AUBERGINE PIE

Cut several aubergines (you will need 4 or 5 depending on size) into long slices, about ¼ inch thick; flour them, dip them in beaten egg, then coat them generously with breadcrumbs. Fry each slice in a pan with oil until the outside is crisp and brown. Have a large shallow fireproof dish well buttered and arrange half of the slices at the bottom of the dish.

Cut enough slices of Double Gloucester cheese to cover each aubergine slice, and put them on it.

Make a thick tomato sauce from a 14-oz (397-g) tin of tomatoes, a glass of red wine, a tablespoon of tomato *purée*, a teaspoon of dried basil and 5 crushed cloves of garlic. Let the sauce simmer for 15 minutes.

Pour the sauce over the cheese and aubergine slices, so that it covers them completely. Now dot the sauce generously with blobs of cream cheese, or with layers of Mozzarella or Bel Paese, then place on top the remaining breadcrumbed aubergine slices in a layer.

Sprinkle enough grated Parmesan over the top to cover the slices, and bake for 15 minutes in the oven, preheated to 400°F/200°C/Gas Mark 6. This is a substantial but very delicious dinner dish.

CAULIFLOWER CHEESE

This might seem prosaic after the above excesses, but though this is a commonly-known and loved dish, it is very rare for it to be cooked really successfully rather than just adequately. The trick is to cook it within 5 minutes and to assemble and serve it at once, for it is essential that the cauliflower be *al dente*. It can easily be done within this time if all the ingredients are prepared in advance: the cauliflower sliced, the cheese grated, and the milk, butter and seasoning near to hand. It cannot be cooked in advance and then reheated, nor can it be left in the oven for unpunctual guests.

Slice the cauliflower into sprigs, including with each floret a part of the central stem. Use as much of the outside leaves as is edible raw – bite a bit to see whether or not a leaf is fibrous. Plunge the sprigs and leaves into a wide saucepan with an inch of boiling water. Arrange the pieces so that the stems lie in the water with the florets above. Let it cook vigorously for 2 minutes and then drain it, leaving the cauliflower in a colander with a lid on it, over the saucepan, so that any more water will drain away. Alternatively, you can steam the cauliflower, but that will take longer.

Make the *Cheese Sauce* (see page 28) while the cauliflower is cooking and finish it off while the cauliflower is having an extra half minute to drain, but not to lose heat. Tip the cauliflower into a buttered *tian*, pour the sauce over it, sprinkle the top with a few breadcrumbs, place it under a very hot grill for a minute, then serve.

1 **Cauliflower Cream Cheese**
This and the next recipe are variations on the *Cauliflower Cheese* above, and are lighter and more delicate dishes.

In the liquidizer, blend 8 oz (225 g) of cream cheese with ½ pint (300 ml) of single cream; add a pinch of nutmeg and salt and pepper. Heat the mixture slowly, stirring all the time. Have 2 egg yolks in a bowl, pour in a little of the hot sauce, mix them together, then pour the egg mixture back into the saucepan and reheat it without letting it boil. When the sauce thickens, pour it over the well-drained, *al dente* cauliflower (prepared as for the *Cauliflower Cheese*) and place it under a hot grill for a moment.

2 **Cauliflower with Cream and Parmesan**
Heat ½ pint (300 ml) of single cream with seasoning and nutmeg, pour it over the well-drained, lightly-cooked cauliflower (see *Cauliflower Cheese*), sprinkle the top with 6 oz (175 g) of grated Parmesan and place the dish under a hot grill until the Parmesan has melted.

OEUFS FLORENTINES

Instead of using the usual cheese sauce that can make this dish rather heavy and filling, try the sauce from the *Cauliflower with Cream and Parmesan*, above.

1 lb (450 g) spinach
4 poached eggs
2 oz (50 g) butter
½ pt (300 ml) single cream
salt and pepper
pinch of nutmeg
4 oz (100 g) grated Parmesan

Tear the spinach leaves into small pieces and cook them in the butter until reduced by a third. Pour off the liquid and keep it for soup. Ensure that the yolks of the poached eggs are uncooked and the whites just set. Chop the spinach with a wooden spoon and place it in a well-buttered fireproof dish. Slip the poached eggs on top of the spinach.

Heat the cream with the salt, pepper and nutmeg, pour it carefully over the eggs and spinach, sprinkle the top with the Parmesan and place the dish under a hot grill for no longer than a minute. If the yolks are set, the dish is ruined.

ONION TART

Make a short-crust pastry shell with butter and bake it blind in a hot oven for 10 minutes. Meanwhile, *sauté* ½ lb (225 g) of sliced onions in 2 oz (50 g) of butter until soft. Mix the onions with ½ pint (300 ml) of single cream and salt, pepper and a pinch of nutmeg. Pour it into the pastry shell and bake it in a preheated 375°F/190°C/Gas Mark 5 oven for 20 minutes.

GOURMET VEGETABLE PIE

short-cut pastry
1 aubergine
egg, flour and breadcrumbs for the aubergine
oil
3 tbsp *Tomato Sauce* (see page 140)
4 tbsp chopped onion
3 oz (75 g) grated Double Gloucester cheese
¼ pt (150 ml) single cream
8 oz (225 g) cooked Jerusalem artichokes
4 tbsp *Garlic Cream* (see page 29)
2 oz (50 g) grated Parmesan

Slice the aubergine in half, then cut it across in slices about ½ inch thick. Flour, egg and breadcrumb each slice and fry them in oil until the breadcrumbs are crisp and brown. Lay these pieces at the bottom of a fireproof dish and spoon the *Tomato Sauce* over them. Now sprinkle 2 tablespoons of the onion over the sauce, then the Double Gloucester and pour the cream over the cheese, so that it goes into a layer and does not sink to the bottom of the dish. A little will, but if you have fitted the aubergines in well not too much will seep down. Season.

Now add the Jerusalem artichokes in another layer, sprinkle those with the rest of the onion and cover them with the *Garlic Cream*. Season again. Sprinkle the Parmesan over the *Garlic Cream*, and cover the top with pastry. Brush it with beaten egg and bake it in an oven preheated to 400°F/200°C/Gas Mark 6 for 45 minutes or until the crust is quite brown.

GARLIC CREAM TART

> short-crust pastry
> 50 cloves of garlic
> ½ lb (225 g) potatoes
> 1 tbsp olive oil
> salt and pepper
> ¼ pt (150 ml) *Garlic Cream* (see page 29)
> ¼ pt (150 ml) single cream

Bake the pastry blind in a shallow dish for 10 minutes.

Peel the garlic by pouring boiling water on the cloves to loosen their skins, and peel and slice the potatoes into ¼-inch thick pieces. *Sauté* the garlic cloves in the olive oil, then add the potatoes with the salt and pepper. Cook them together, turning the garlic and potatoes so that they will soak up the oil. Then pour in a pint (600 ml) of boiling water and let the mixture boil for 15 minutes. Drain the liquid off and reserve it for stock. Put the cooked potato and garlic over the bottom of the tart, mix the cream with the *Garlic Cream* and pour this over the top. Bake in a preheated 400°F/200°C/Gas Mark 6 oven for 15 minutes.

GREEN PEPPER AND MARROW TARKARI

Slice 4 green peppers, then peel a small vegetable marrow and cube the flesh. Cook them together in a little vegetable oil over a low heat for 7 minutes. Add 2 chopped green chillies, a teaspoon each of turmeric powder, *garam masala* and cumin seeds, and the juice of a lemon.

Season it with salt and black pepper. Raise the heat and shake the vegetables and spices together for about 2 minutes or until they brown and begin to stick to the pan.

CABBAGE TARKARI

Slice a small white cabbage, 2 onions and a ginger root. Cook these in a little vegetable oil over a low heat for 7 minutes. Add a teaspoon each of turmeric and *garam masala*, paprika and a pinch of cinnamon with salt, pepper and the juice of a lemon. Raise the heat and shake the cabbage and spices together for a moment and serve.

CABBAGE WITH COCONUT

Heat a little vegetable oil in a pan and in it cook 1 sliced onion, 1 sliced ginger root, 3 crushed cloves of garlic and a teaspoon of paprika for a minute or so, until the onion begins to turn soft.

Slice a small cabbage thinly and add it to the pan. Turn the heat up and stir-fry until the cabbage has lost its bulk by a third, but is still *al dente*. Finally, add 3 oz (75 g) of grated coconut. Shake the pan, stir and serve immediately.

BAKED VEGETABLES WITH YOGHURT PASTE

Slice a cauliflower into small pieces. Peel a marrow, slice it in half lengthways and scoop out the flesh. Put the cauliflower pieces inside the marrow, pour over the *Yoghurt Paste* (see page 157, recipe for *Spiced Potatoes*) and place it in a casserole dish. Cook it in a preheated medium oven for 30 minutes.

For this, try to find a dish that the marrow will fit into snugly. If you cannot, then cut the marrow into large cubes and put the cauliflower on it. Either way make sure that the paste covers each piece of vegetable.

JERUSALEM ARTICHOKES

These are cheap and are probably the most delicious root vegetables of all. Do not peel them. Cut the large ones or break them with your hands. Scrub the outer skin with a brush beneath a running cold tap – this will remove all the dirt and mud. Boil them in salted water for about 15–20 minutes. Reserve some for soup, with their water, if you have more than you need for whatever dish you are preparing.

ARTICHAUTS PROVENÇALE

1 lb (450 g) boiled Jerusalem artichokes (see instructions above)
1 lb (450 g) peeled fresh tomatoes
1 head of garlic
3 tbsp olive oil
salt and pepper
handful of chopped basil
¼ lb (100 g) Mozzarella cheese
breadcrumbs

Pour boiling water over the cloves of garlic and the tomatoes and peel them both. Chop both coarsely, add them to the olive oil in a pan with the salt and pepper, and cook for a few moments. Then add the well-drained artichokes and the basil. Turn the mixture into a casserole and place it in a preheated medium oven for half an hour. Cut the cheese into strips and place these on top of the mixture; sprinkle breadcrumbs over the lot and put it back into the oven at a higher heat until the breadcrumbs are brown – about 15 minutes.

ARTICHOKES IN SWEET-AND-SOUR SAUCE

1 lb (450 g) cooked Jerusalem artichokes
Sweet-and-sour Sauce (see page 26)
¼ lb (100 g) broken walnuts
1 tbsp sultanas
¼ lb (100 g) cream cheese

Heat the sauce, stir in the walnuts, then add the artichokes and the sultanas. Tip the mixture into a small fireproof dish or casserole and place it uncovered in a preheated medium oven after dotting the top with spoonfuls of the cream cheese. Leave it for 20 minutes or until the cheese has melted and run.

ARTICHOKES WITH GINGER AND CHEESE

Grate 1 ginger root and *sauté* it in a tablespoon of olive oil. Add 1 lb (450 g) of hot cooked artichokes, sprinkle them with Parmesan cheese and place them under a hot grill.

RATATOUILLE

This is possibly one of the most famous of all vegetable dishes. The combination of vegetables should be cooked slowly in olive oil and left for a day so that all the flavours are well fused, before reheating it or cating it cold. In the Mediterranean one can make this dish in the spring when the first aubergines and peppers start to appear. In Britain though, the months to make it are July and August, when those imported vegetables are cheap to buy because the Mediterranean countries then have a glut of them.

1 lb (450 g) aubergines
1 lb (450 g) courgettes
1 lb (450 g) green or red peppers
1 lb (450 g) onions
5 cloves of garlic
3 tbsp olive oil
1 lb (450 g) tomatoes
salt and pepper
handful of fresh basil or parsley

Do not skin either the aubergines or the courgettes, but slice them in ¼-inch pieces and then quarter each piece. Place them in a colander, sprinkle salt over them and leave them for 2 hours so that they will lose some of their water content. Chop the onions and the peppers, squeeze the garlic and allow all the vegetables to *sauté* in the olive oil in a covered pan for about 40 minutes.

If you make this dish in the Mediterranean, then you can use fresh tomatoes, but I can see no point in wasting the flavour of home-grown British ones in this dish. Thus, I would use a tin of tomatoes, but would make certain that I had squeezed all the moisture from them. Add the tomatoes and let them amalgamate with the rest of the vegetables, then season them to taste with salt and pepper. Leave it for a day and, before serving, stir in the fresh herbs.

PIPÉRADE

This is a cousin of *ratatouille*, and when it is well cooked and the eggs permeate the peppers, it becomes a light, frothy *purée* and is delicious. There are, however, three problems here. Firstly, the peppers ought to be small, because if large the fibrous tissue of the outer skin loosens in the cooking and becomes not only unattractive (like damp strips of cellophane), but also quite indigestible. The next and almost insoluble problem concerns the tomatoes. Bought tomatoes are unsatisfactory for the dish, but home-grown ones are so excellent that I feel it is a crime to disguise their clear flavour. Thus, one is left with tinned tomatoes. The other vegetables are strong enough to disguise that slight tin flavour, but the real problem is coping with the liquid left within the pulp of these tomatoes, even after they are drained. Finally, the peppers and onions should not lose too much of their water content, for even when the eggs amalgamate with the oil and the vegetables, they will reject the moisture. Then, however carefully it is served, it will still look unpalatable.

6 small green or red peppers or a mixture of both
4 onions
1 14-oz (397-g) tin of tomatoes
2 crushed cloves of garlic
2 tbsp olive oil
salt and pepper
4 eggs

Take the stems and seeds from the peppers and cut the peppers and onions into thin slices. Pour the olive oil into a thick-bottomed shallow pan (a copper frying pan is perfect because it retains the heat so well), add the garlic, peppers and onions, season and simmer gently, uncovered. Don't hurry this stage; allow at least half an hour for the peppers and onions to slowly soften, and stir them occasionally to stop them sticking to the pan. If a *purée* is desired, they can be left to cool and placed in the blender for a second, but I don't consider it necessary.

Now, add the well-drained tomatoes, squeezing them dry in your fist first (the only effective manner). Stir them into the mixture, taste it and correct the seasoning. Then quickly add the eggs and, using a fork, beat them into the mixture so that it begins to rise in the pan. Serve at once. This is excellent with hot garlic bread.

CREAMED CUCUMBERS

Eliza Acton, in 1845, gave several recipes for cooking cucumbers and, in France today, the tradition persists. Yet this is one vegetable which we obstinately think must be eaten raw.

3 cucumbers
2 chopped onions
salt and pepper
3 dsp butter
½ pt (300 ml) cream
handful of chopped parsley or basil

Peel the cucumbers, halve them down their length, scoop out the seeds, sprinkle the inside with salt and leave them to drain for 1 hour. Then wash the salt off them underneath the cold tap. Slice them in 3-inch lengths about 1½ inches wide. Melt the butter and soften the onions in it for a moment before adding the cucumber. Season and leave over a gentle heat in a covered pan for about 45 minutes. Add the cream, stir well until it is hot, then throw in the parsley or basil. Serve at once.

1 **Baked Cucumbers with Cream Sauce**

After the cucumbers have been prepared, salted and drained, wash them beneath a cold tap and place them in a *tian* with 3 dessertspoons of melted butter, and salt and pepper. Then place the dish in a preheated oven at a medium heat and leave it for an hour. The cucumbers will hardly colour and though the inside should be tender, the outside should now be crisp. Have ready a cheese sauce and pour it over the baked cucumbers; then place the dish under a hot grill to brown.

CUCUMBERS FRIED IN EGG AND BREADCRUMBS

Quarter the cucumbers lengthways, then slice them into 3-inch strips. Salt them, leave them for an hour in a colander to drain, then pat them dry with a cloth. Dip each piece in flour, then in beaten egg and lastly in breadcrumbs, coating the surface well. Fry them in butter or oil for a few minutes, turning them so that the pieces are nicely browned and the breadcrumbs crisp.

COURGETTES

Never skin these. Small courgettes can be cooked whole and need to be boiled in salted water for no longer than 3 minutes. Larger courgettes can be sliced across in 2-inch lengths and cooked in the same manner. They should never be soggy, but firm enough to be sliced on the plate with a knife.

FRIED COURGETTES

This is a common method of cooking this vegetable in restaurants. The courgettes are sliced into thin discs, then either floured or put into a thin batter and fried in a pan with a little hot oil in it. The cooking time is minimal – not more than a minute – or until flour or batter has just become crisp.

The point to remember with these is that the batter must be thin and light; crisp curls of heavy batter around a little bit of courgette are very off-putting.

ITALIAN FRIED COURGETTES

Cut the courgettes into strips like small chip potatoes, sprinkle salt over them and leave them to drain for an hour. Dry them in a cloth, place them in a bowl with a little flour, salt and pepper, and turn them around with your hands so that each piece is covered with the flour. Fry them in deep oil. When the oil is hot enough, the courgettes will cook within 2 minutes.

COURGETTES IN SWEET-AND-SOUR SAUCE

Cut the courgettes into discs, but not too thinly, and *sauté* them in olive oil for about 3 minutes, stirring the pan so that they all cook evenly. Add ¼ pint (150 ml) of the *Sweet-and-sour Sauce* (see page 26) and let them stew in that for a further 2 minutes before serving.

BUTTERED SPINACH

This is possibly the best way of eating spinach, but you must be prepared to use an enormous amount of butter.

After washing say 2 lb (1 kg) of spinach, shake it dry or pat it dry with a cloth. Put it into a saucepan over a very low heat and stir it for about 5 minutes – or until all the spinach has softened and reduced itself to about ¾ lb (350 g). Put the spinach into a colander and squeeze out any moisture. Reserve any liquid for stock.

Melt 6 oz (175 g) of butter in the saucepan and return the spinach to it. Stir it with a wooden spoon and almost grind the leaves into the butter as it cooks. The spinach will soon soak up all the butter. Turn it out of the pan and put it into the refrigerator.

The next day, repeat the cooking process. Use another 6 oz (175 g) of butter and cook it until the spinach has soaked it all up. It should take only 3 minutes once the butter is hot.

On the third day, add again 6 oz (175 g) of butter and season the spinach with salt and pepper. It will then still be *en branche* but a slight *purée* as well. Once the spinach has soaked up the butter on the first day, it never reduces further in bulk.

1 **Spinach Croquettes**
After the spinach has been cooked and drained as in the first stage of *Buttered Spinach*, above, chop it further with the edge of a wooden spoon while it is still in the colander; then put the spinach in a mixing bowl.

Add 1 beaten egg, 2 oz (50 g) of Parmesan or Sage Derby cheese (the latter goes particularly well with spinach), salt, pepper and a pinch of nutmeg. Sprinkle a little flour on a board and roll the mixture into small cakes. Next, roll them in breadcrumbs. Fry the croquettes in hot olive oil.

2 **Spinach with Cream**
After the spinach has been cooked, drained and chopped (as above), turn it into a buttered *tian*. Heat $\frac{1}{2}$ pint (300 ml) of single cream seasoned with salt, pepper and a pinch of sugar. Pour the cream over the spinach and place it under a hot grill until the spinach and cream begin to heave and bubble.

NEW CARROTS

If they are new and small, carrots need only scrubbing and boiling in enough water to cover them. For 1 lb (450 g) of carrots use 2 oz (50 g) of butter, a pinch of salt and a pinch of sugar. Cook them with the lid off the pan until they have absorbed all of the water, by which time they should be tender. Add more butter and black pepper, and shake the pan. Serve them with a little chopped parsley over them.

GLAZED CARROTS

Larger and tougher carrots need to be cut diagonally into thin
discs, boiled, as with the new carrots, in enough water to
cover them and with 2 oz (50 g) of butter and a pinch each
of salt and sugar. When they are tender (in about 15–20
minutes), add 2 teaspoons of brown sugar and another 2 oz
(50 g) of butter. Shake the pan and stir the carrots until the
sugar has melted and has covered the carrots. If kept warm
for 5–10 minutes in the oven in a fireproof dish, they will
become more glazed.

1   **Carrots with Cream**
Instead of adding the extra butter and sugar, as in the
above recipe, pour ¼ pint (150 ml) of single cream over the
carrots and heat them until the cream begins to thicken.
Again, they may be kept warm for 5–10 minutes in the oven
without spoiling.

CARROT PUFFS

'Scrape and boil them and mash them very fine, add to every
pint of the pulp about ½ pint of bread crumb, some eggs, four
whites to the pint, a nutmeg grated, some orange flower
water, sugar to taste, a little sack, and mix it with thick cream.
They must be fried in rendered suet very hot.' That is an
eighteenth-century English recipe; the following one is a
modern version. These puffs are far more delicious than they
might sound. Boil 1 lb (450 g) sliced carrots; drain, then mash
them. Add the juice from one orange, the yolks of 2 eggs and
enough breadcrumbs to bind the mixture. Then fold in the
whipped whites of the eggs.

Have a little olive oil in a pan, and when it is hot enough,
mould the mixture with your fingers into puffs the shape and
size of a ping-pong ball. Drop these into the oil and roll them
around in the pan until they are brown and crisp on the
outside. Pile them on a dish and serve them at once. They
should be crunchy on the outside and light in the centre.

CARROTS WITH MARSALA

Cut 1 lb (450 g) of carrots lengthways into slices – each carrot may be cut into 8 pieces. Melt 2 oz (50 g) of butter in a pan and add the carrots, stirring constantly so that they begin to soak up the butter. Then season them and pour in a glass of marsala. Simmer them for 3 minutes and cover them with boiling water. Place a lid on the pan and let them stew until they are tender – about 15 minutes. Take the lid from the pan, turn up the heat and reduce what liquid there is to about 1 tablespoon.

BEETROOTS

Small ones are delicious hot, served with a cream sauce. Boil 1 lb (450 g) in their skins, take each one out of the water with a fork when cooked, and peel them with a knife; the skin comes off very easily. Place the beetroots in a buttered *tian* and pour over them a sauce made by mixing ¼ pint (150 ml) of single cream with salt, pepper and a pinch of nutmeg. The sauce can be thickened more by adding a raw egg yolk to it. Alternatively, some people prefer to serve the beetroots in a light *sauce Béchamel*.

1 **Beetroots with Parsley and Breadcrumbs**
After the beetroots have been boiled and peeled, put them back into a pan with a tablespoon of olive oil. Season them and let them cook in the oil for a couple of minutes. Chop a handful of parsley and mix it with 3 tablespoons of breadcrumbs, add these to the pan and let the oil and the beetroot juice soak up the breadcrumbs. Garnish them with chopped spring onions.
Turnips may be cooked in the same way.

2 **Beetroots with Garlic Cream**
Larger cooked and peeled beetroots can be cut in slices, laid in a buttered *tian* and have about ¼ pint (150 ml) of *Garlic Cream* (see page 29) poured over them. Then place the *tian* in the oven for 5 minutes to warm. The cream will go pink, but is rather attractive.

187

RED CABBAGE WITH CHESTNUTS

1 sliced red cabbage
½ lb (225 g) dried chestnuts
1 lb (450 g) cooking apples
10 cloves of garlic
½ tsp ground bay leaf, clove, nutmeg and mace
2 glasses red wine
1 tbsp olive oil
salt and pepper

Pour boiling water over the chestnuts and leave them in it to treble in bulk. It will take about an hour. Peel and dice the cooking apples.

Use an iron casserole with a tight lid; the dish should be usable in the oven as well as on top of the stove. Heat the olive oil in the casserole and crush the garlic and the spices into it. Then add the cabbage and turn it so that it is coated with the oil. Add the apples and the chestnuts, then the wine and ¼ pint (150 ml) of boiling water. Stir the ingredients together well and place the casserole in the oven at a low heat. Leave it for 3–4 hours.

This is one dish that is always improved by being cooked the day before it is eaten, left to cool and reheated the next day.

RED CABBAGE WITH SWEET-AND-SOUR SAUCE

Slice one cabbage thinly, put it into a casserole and pour over it ½ pint (300 ml) of *Sweet-and-sour Sauce* (see page 26). Let it cook in a slow oven for 3 hours.

PAPRIKA CABBAGE

Make a cold marinade out of a tablespoon of paprika, a teaspoon each of ground caraway and coriander, salt, pepper, the juice of a lemon and half a cup of wine vinegar. Slice a white cabbage thinly across its shape horizontally, so that one has diminishing circles, and leave it in the marinade for a day. Heat a pan with a little oil in it and stir-fry the cabbage for 2 minutes. Then add a tablespoon of the marinade and fry it for another minute. Take from the heat and mix in onions, as on page 18.

TOMATES À LA PROVENÇALE

I cannot resist giving this recipe, for it is excellent when made with large, very fresh tomatoes. They must be at least 3 inches in diameter.

4 large tomatoes
5 crushed cloves of garlic
2 tbsp chopped spring onions
2 tbsp chopped parsley or basil
2 tbsp olive oil
2 oz (50 g) breadcrumbs
salt and pepper

Remove the stems and cut the tomatoes in half across their middles. Either gently press out the flesh and seeds with your hands or cut it out with a grapefruit knife. Place the scooped-out flesh in a bowl and season the insides of the shells with salt and pepper.

Combine all of the other ingredients, except the breadcrumbs, with the tomato pulp, stirring well. Cover the bowl and leave it for 30 minutes, then fill the tomato shells with the stuffing and arrange them in an oiled dish. Sprinkle the breadcrumbs over the tomatoes. Put them at the top of a very hot oven and bake them for 10–15 minutes or until the breadcrumbs are brown on top.

FASOULIA

This is a famous Greek dish made from haricot beans.

Use ½ lb (225 g) of dried haricot beans. Pour boiling water over them and repeat the process three times within an hour as described on page 32. Drain them, then heat ¼ pint (150 ml) of olive oil in a thick-bottomed saucepan. Throw in the beans with 10 cloves of garlic, a bay leaf, a pinch of thyme, sage and a teaspoon of oregano. Let the mixture simmer in the oil for 10–15 minutes, and add enough boiling water to cover the beans by almost an inch. Stir in 2 tablespoons of tomato *purée*.

Turn the mixture out into a casserole and cook it in the oven at a low heat for 3 hours. If the heat on top of the stove is gentle enough, they may be left there to simmer quietly. Season them, when cooked, with sea salt and black pepper, then pour over them the juice from a lemon and sprinkle them with some chopped raw onion. Serve either hot or cold.

BROAD BEANS

When very young, broad beans can be boiled in their pods in salted water for about 3 minutes and the whole vegetable eaten plain. When they are large and tougher, they may be treated in other ways, such as the following ones.

BROAD BEANS IN YOGHURT SAUCE

1 lb (450 g) broad beans
3 oz (75 g) lentils
2 cloves of garlic
½ pt (300 ml) yoghurt
1 egg yolk
chopped parsley

Soak the lentils and cook them in about ¾ pint (450 ml) of boiling water for 15 minutes. Allow them to cool and blend them to a *purée*. Boil the broad beans in water for about 10 minutes or until they are tender. Crush the garlic into the yoghurt, beat in the egg yolk and add the lentil *purée*. Pour the mixture over the drained broad beans and heat gently until the sauce becomes thick. Garnish with the parsley and serve.

BROAD BEANS COOKED IN STOCK

Use 1 pint (600 ml) of the *White Vegetable Stock* (see page 45) and 1 oz (25 g) of butter for cooking 1 lb (450 g) of broad beans. When the beans are tender, pour off the stock into a bowl containing 2 egg yolks and the juice from 1 lemon. Mix these together well and return them to the pan, cooking them gently and without boiling until the sauce begins to thicken. Pour it over the beans and serve.

FAISCEDDA

This comes from Sardinia and is made from fresh broad beans, when they are plentiful, from February to May, they are cooked thus in a *tian* over an open fire. However, fresh broad beans in Britain are so delicious that I would alter my rule and use at any time of the year 1 lb (450 g) of frozen broad beans. Unlike most frozen vegetables, the broad bean's flavour is not diminished to a large extent.

Cook the vegetables in water, drain them, then put them through the mincer. The Sardinian method is to mix in 2 teaspoons of sugar, a handful of breadcrumbs, a pinch of nutmeg and cinnamon and 4 eggs, then to form the mixture into a flat cake and to fry it in oil on both sides until it is crisp and like a rather obstinate and formidable pancake. I omit the sugar, separate the eggs and, using 2 extra whites, whip the combined whites hard and fold them into the mixture just before cooking. Fry it in oil and cut it like a cake while it is still warm. If, like *falafels*, the mixture is cooked as separate little cakes, they make a suitable appetizer.

RUNNER BEANS WITH TOMATO AND GARLIC

Top and tail 1 lb (450 g) of runner beans and pare the string off the sides with a sharp knife. Slice them into 1-inch lengths and cook them in boiling salted water for no more than 4 minutes. Drain them. Put a tablespoon of olive oil into a pan, add 3 crushed cloves of garlic and 5 peeled and chopped tomatoes (home-grown, if possible). Add the drained beans to the pan and let them cook gently in the mixture for 5 minutes with the lid on so that the tomatoes turn into a *purée*.

LETTUCE COOKED IN BUTTER AND BREADCRUMBS

Cos is one of the best lettuces for cooking. Wash the leaves and tear them into small pieces. Melt 1 oz (25 g) of butter in a pan and throw in the lettuce. Stir-fry it for 2 minutes; the lettuce will lose its bulk by half. Season it and add a tablespoon of breadcrumbs and 1 crushed clove of garlic; stir it for another minute.

Serve it with chopped spring onion, parsley or mint on top. The lettuce must not lose too much of its moisture and the stalks should certainly still be *al dente*, so watch the vegetable with care.

PARSNIPS

This is a very British vegetable, which is possibly why *haute cuisine* has disdained it. Parsnips have been eaten here since the Middle Ages, and the green tops were fed to cows as late as the nineteenth century, as it was thought that they enriched the milk. From Elizabethan days onwards, there are many recipes that use them in puddings, because their sweetness was much liked and it mingled well with honey. In France today, while much attention is given to the turnip, as in *navets glacés*, the superior parsnip is ignored.

Parsnips need very little cooking, but must be par-boiled first, before any further stage of cooking. Small ones can be scraped and scrubbed clean, then cooked whole, but larger ones have a central core that is harder than the flesh around it. They are best cut down the centre and quartered – or they can be cut diagonally in the Chinese manner. They can also be chopped into small dice. The boiling time depends on the way they are sliced: diced, they will take 3 minutes; sliced diagonally, 5 minutes; and cut into quarters, 7 minutes.

GLAZED PARSNIPS

As they are a dry vegetable, parsnips will soak up a lot of oil, butter or cream, but this means that they are very satisfactory for absorbing other flavours.

1 lb (450 g) parsnips
a bit more than 4 oz (100 g) butter
1 tbsp brown sugar
1 tsp crushed cloves
1 tsp caraway seeds
salt and pepper

Dice the parsnips, boil them for 3 minutes in salted water and drain them well. Mix together the sugar, cloves and caraway. Return the parsnips to the saucepan, melt the butter over them, shaking the pan as you do so, then add the sugar and spices and a little more seasoning. Cook for a further 3 minutes with the pan covered. They should have then soaked up all the butter, so add an extra bit and serve. These can be kept warm in the oven, but then you must add even more butter, as, like spinach, they will soak up as much as you give them.

PARSNIPS IN CURRY SAUCE

1 lb (450 g) parsnips
½ pt (300 ml) *Curry Sauce* (see page 25)

Quarter the parsnips and boil them for 7 minutes; drain them well. Lay them in a buttered *tian* and pour the *Curry Sauce*, heated, over them. Place them in a preheated oven at a medium heat and leave them for 30 minutes.

Jane Grigson, in *Good Things*,* gives an excellent recipe for *Parsnip Curry Soup* and another for boiled parsnips glazed in orange sauce and brown sugar. Excellent. Try also parsnips cooked as in this recipe but with *Sweet-and-sour Sauce* (see page 26) instead of the *Curry Sauce*.

PANAIS À LA PROVENÇALE

1 lb (450 g) parsnips
1 lb (450 g) fresh tomatoes
1 head of crushed cloves of garlic
2 tbsp olive oil
salt and pepper
handful of basil or parsley

Dice the parsnips and boil them for 3 minutes; drain them. Peel the tomatoes and the garlic by pouring water over them; then drain and peel both. Chop them coarsely. Heat the oil in a saucepan; add the tomatoes, garlic, parsnips and seasoning. Leave them over a low heat for 10 minutes, then add the basil or parsley.

PARSNIPS WITH MUSHROOMS AND CREAM

Dice 1 lb (450 g) parsnips and boil them for 3 minutes. In a separate pan, place 1 lb (450 g) sliced field mushrooms with 3 oz (75 g) of butter, and salt and pepper; let them simmer for 3 minutes or until the mushroom juices have begun to seep. Add the parsnips to the mushrooms, cover them and let them cook for a further 2 minutes. Have a buttered *tian* ready, pour the vegetables into this and over them pour ¼ pint (150 ml) of single cream. Put them in a preheated oven for 15 minutes at 350°F/180°C/Gas Mark 4 heat.

* *Good Things*, Jane Grigson, Michael Joseph, London, 1971.

PURÉE OF PARSNIPS WITH GARLIC CREAM

Dice 1 lb (450 g) of parsnips and boil them – this time for 7 minutes. Drain them, then mash them with 2 oz (50 g) of butter, and salt and pepper. When they have soaked up all the butter, add ¼ pint (150 ml) of *Garlic Cream* (see page 29). Put them in a fireproof dish and place them under a hot grill for a few minutes.

This can also be used as a filling in pancakes or as a flavouring in a *timbale* (see page 84).

1 Parsnip Tart

Parsnips are very good in tarts and pies. Make a short-crust pastry shell with butter and bake it blind in a hot oven for 10 minutes. Over the bottom of the pastry shell, pour in the above quantity of *Purée of Parsnips with Garlic Cream*, above.

Slice 1 lb (450 g) of onions, *sauté* them in 2 oz (50 g) of butter until soft, take them from the heat and stir in 2 tablespoons of double cream, with salt, pepper and 2 egg yolks. Pour this over the *purée*. Sprinkle the top with grated Parmesan or Double Gloucester cheese and bake the tart in a preheated 400°F/200°C/Gas Mark 6 oven for 30 minutes.

2 Parsnip Croquettes

Into the *Parsnip Purée with Garlic Cream*, beat 1 egg yolk, 2 oz (50 g) of grated Parmesan and 2 tablespoons of breadcrumbs. Refrigerate this for an hour, then beat in 2 whipped egg whites. Fry dessertspoon sized pieces of the mixture in hot oil, turning them over with a spatula as soon as the bottom side is brown.

CHICORY

This excellent winter vegetable which we import from Belgium is disliked by some people when cooked because of its bitterness. Chicory need not be bitter and, if it is, that grave state has been caused by the chemical reaction between the vegetable and the knife used on it. When cutting it or taking out its core, use only a silver or stainless steel knife.

CHICORY WITH CREAM SAUCE

This recipe uses every bit of the vegetable and the liquid that
it has been cooked in as well. Slice the 5 or 6 chicory plants
across into 1-inch pieces and drop it into a saucepan with a
little butter. Let it cook slowly in its own steam – it will be
done within 5 minutes. Drain the chicory and keep the liquid.
Place the vegetable into a *tian*, make a *roux* with 1 oz (25 g)
of butter and 1 oz (25 g) of flour, season it with salt and pepper
and add half a pint (300 ml) of single cream and the chicory
liquid to it. Stir it over a gentle flame and pour the sauce over
the chicory, then place it quickly under a hot grill to brown.

PEKING VEGETABLES

Choose with care the three or four vegetables to cook by this
method. All must be in perfect condition and have roughly
the same water content. It is no good serving a dish which has
two vegetables that are crunchy, while the other two are limp
like shredded blotting paper. Some might suggest that the
vegetables like spinach and leek can be added for a moment
at the very last, but though this is so, there is the risk that the
miscellany of flavours is too baffling for the palate. Remember
also to use only that part of the vegetable that you would eat
raw anyway. It is no good thinking you can magically alter
fibrous roughage into a delicacy. Choose, for example, the
inside sticks from celery, the inside leaves of the Florentine
fennel or celeriac, or the yellow heart of the Savoy cabbage.

Wash or chop all the vegetables and have them ready by the
pan before you begin cooking. Heat a very thin film of olive oil
in a wok or heavy pan – a little more oil than you would use in
pancakes, but not much. When you see the smoke beginning
to rise from the oil, drop the vegetables in and turn them about
quickly with a wooden fork. Stir-fry them (see page 116) for
3 minutes and no longer, then add a tablespoon of soy sauce
and, in the cloud of steam that rises, go on stirring for another
minute. If a vegetable sticks, take the pan from the heat at
once. Should you find that there is too much liquid, then you
have cooked them for too long. The vegetables should have
sucked up the soy sauce and should be still almost raw and dry.
Sprinkle them with chopped spring onion and serve at once.

Do not be under the impression that you can keep them hot in the oven: the vegetables will simply cook and be ruined. This is a dish that has to be made at the time that you and your guests are ready to eat.

The Chinese would also add, when the soy sauce is poured in, two flavouring powders. The first would be a seasoned salt in the form of a type of monosodium glutamate, and the second, a good teaspoon of five-spice powder or *satay* powder. The five-spice powder is made from orange peel, aniseed, fennel, cassia, clove and ginger, while the *satay* powder is made from spices and peanuts. They do alter the vegetables' flavour into something quite else, which can be delicious.

HOT-MARINATED VEGETABLES IN BATTER

First choose the vegetables you want and judge, depending on whether they are hard or soft, how long they must be cooked in the marinade. Parsnips and carrots need 8 minutes; swedes and turnips, 6 minutes; and a cubed aubergine, a quartered pepper and sprigs of cauliflower, 2 minutes. It is, however, almost impossible to dictate exact times, because much depends upon the quality of the vegetable and on how large the pieces are. The point is that they must emerge from the marinade softened on the surface but raw in the centre.

Mushrooms may be done in the same way, but they cannot be hot-marinated. Instead, they should be left whole in the cold marinade for a day before being drained and battered.

Hot Marinade (see page 115)
2 oz (50 g) flour
1 tsp olive oil
1 egg yolk
salt and pepper
6 tbsp milk – or water if you want the batter to be extremely light
2 stiffly-whipped egg whites
chopped spring onions

Plunge the prepared vegetables into the boiling hot marinade and cook them for the time that their size and texture dictates. Drain them and let them cool.

To make a light batter, mix the flour with the oil and the

egg yolk into a paste, and add the seasoning. Then stir in the milk or water and finally fold in the egg whites. Dip each piece of vegetable into the batter and fry it in oil in a hot pan. Sprinkle them with chopped spring onions and serve them hot, at once. The Chinese would deep fry these vegetables, but I can rarely afford that amount of oil; shallow frying works but you have to turn the vegetables.

1 **Sweet-and-sour Vegetables in Batter**
Melt a tablespoon of Barbados sugar in cooking oil. You can use honey, but you will need more than a tablespoonful of it, and it is expensive. Then add ¼ pint (150 ml) of cider vinegar and let it bubble for a moment before adding ¼ pint (150 ml) of *Hot Marinade* (see page 115).

Diagonally-cut 1 lb (450 g) of mixed vegetables and cook them in the *Hot Marinade* for the time specified in the above recipe.

Melt a tablespoon of honey in 1 tablespoon of boiling water, then add the juice of 2 lemons. When the vegetables are cooked enough, take them from the *Hot Marinade* and plunge them into the cold *Sweet-and-sour Marinade* on page 116, turning them over so that each piece is coated. Allow them to cool in this sauce. Make the light batter as for the above recipe, cover each piece of vegetable with it and fry the pieces quickly in the oil. Some of the *Hot Marinade* can be added to the cold one, heated up and served with the hot vegetables.

COLD MARINATED MARROW

Our plump vegetable marrows are particularly good cooked in the Chinese manner. The British method of boiling them in discs until they are limp wastes their wonderful flavour and texture. After excess cooking, they always give out more water, and I remember as a child that such cooked marrow was served on a layer of bread to soak up the liquid in the vegetable dish – not a palatable sight.

Peel a medium-sized marrow, then cut it lengthways and dispose of the seeds and the soft core; cut the flesh into cubes about ¾-inch square. Make the cold sweet-and-sour sauce with a tablespoon of honey melted in 1 tablespoon of boiling water and then added to the juice of 2 lemons. Toss the marrow cubes in this and let them marinate for some hours or up to a day in the refrigerator. Grate 1 ginger root, grind a tablespoon of dill seed and let this cook for a couple of minutes in a tablespoon of olive oil before adding the marrow cubes. Raise the heat and stir-fry them (see page 116) for about 3 minutes, so that the marrow is crisp and slightly brown on the outside. Add a tablespoon of soy sauce and continue to stir-fry for another half minute or until there is no liquid in the pan.

1 **Marrow with Hot-marinated Vegetables**
This is a splendid mixture. Make it basically the same way as for the *Cold Marinated Marrow*, above, but when the marrow has cooked for 2 minutes, add a variety of hot-marinated vegetables (see page 117) and stir-fry these with the marrow for another 2 minutes before adding the soy sauce. The mixture of different marinades in this dish gives great zest and piquancy. An optional extra is to add chopped nuts – almonds, unsalted peanuts, walnuts – to the pan after the soy sauce has been poured in.

PAKORA

This is an Indian version of vegetables in batter.
To the flour for the batter in the recipe for *Spiced Pancakes* (see page 166), add also a pinch of chilli powder and ¼ teaspoon of *garam masala*. Make the batter with water and no milk, ensuring that it is light. Cover the vegetables in the batter and fry them in a hot oiled pan until the batter is cooked through and crisp.
Vegetables that need little preparation for *Pakora* are whole mushrooms, thick onion rings, the diced stems from cauliflowers, slices of fennel root, the inside crisp leaves of a white cabbage or any diced par-boiled root vegetables.

POACHED BEAN SPROUTS

These are cooked in a saucepan with a tight-fitting lid, in a highly-seasoned stock for only 3 minutes, or until they have shrunk to half their bulk.

1 lb (450 g) bean sprouts
¼ pt (150 ml) *Brown Vegetable Stock* (see page 45)
tsp seasoned seaweed
tsp kelp powder
glass of dry sherry
tsp cornflour
tbsp cold water
black pepper

Mix the seasoned seaweed and kelp powder into the brown stock in a saucepan and bring to the boil. Let it bubble furiously for 1 minute so that the flavours are fused. Add the bean sprouts and the sherry, lower the flame and let the bean sprouts simmer in the hot liquid. After 2 minutes, when their bulk has begun to shrink, turn them over with a wooden spoon and allow the top layer to cook in the stock. They must not be overcooked, but should still be slightly crunchy.

Mix the cornflour with the cold water and add it to the contents in the saucepan. Raise the flame until the stock has thickened and serve at once. No salt is needed, but black pepper can be added at the table.

POACHED BEAN SPROUTS WITH SEAWEED AND MIXED VEGETABLES

Use any variety of dried seaweed for this dish, either *kombu*, *hiziki* or *wakame* – the most common varieties found in health food shops. Use 4 oz (100 g) of the dried weed, pour boiling water over it, leave for an hour, then using the same water boil the seaweed for a further hour. It can now be left in the refrigerator for a day or two. The *kombu* and *wakame* must be chopped into small pieces before being used; the *hiziki*, which looks like shoe laces, needs no cutting.

1 lb (450 g) bean sprouts
4 oz (100 g) dried seaweed
2 large grated carrots
2 large sliced onions
1 finely chopped cucumber
tbsp vegetable oil
¼ pint (150 ml) of *Brown Vegetable Stock* (see page 45)
tsp seasoned seaweed

tsp kelp powder
tsp satay powder
tsp cornflour
tbsp cold water
handful of green tops of spring onions

Drain the stock from the seaweed and reduce it by a third with fast boiling. Add the *Brown Vegetable Stock*, seasoned seaweed, kelp powder and satay powder. Boil for another minute until the flavours are well fused. Reserve this stock.

In the vegetable oil, cook the onions and cucumber in a covered saucepan for 3–5 minutes, shaking the pan in the first minute to ensure that the vegetables do not stick; after that they will happily cook in the liquid given out by the cucumber. Stir in the grated carrots and chopped seaweed and cook for another minute. Now add the bean sprouts and the reserved stock, bring to the boil and let it simmer for another 3 minutes, turning the vegetables over in the last minute. Add the cornflour mixed with the cold water and let the sauce thicken.

The cucumber, carrots and bean sprouts will all be *al dente*. Sprinkle the spring onion tops over the dish before serving.

CHAPTER IX

Savouries, Supper Dishes and Appetizers

An odd combination, yet many of the savouries are a light supper or even a luncheon dish, while if they are made in small pieces or portions, or are sliced into fingers, they can also be the most delicious appetizers.

The savoury which is 'something on toast' has, for the British, become almost a *cliché* for the quick easy supper. Thus, I begin with an assortment of dishes which can be spread on toast and placed under a hot grill.

Experiment by soaking slices of bread first in one of the sauces (but not one with a mayonnaise base), such as the *Tomato Sauce*, the *Green Sauce* with or without horseradish, or the *Sauce Moutarde* (see pages 23–6). Then either fry the bread in hot olive oil until it is crisp or pour a little beaten egg over the bread and grill it until it has browned. These can be sliced into fingers and served as appetizers.

STUFFED EGGS ON TOAST WITH SAUCE À LA CRÈME

Stuff eggs with a cream cheese mixture (see page 92); lightly toast bread, place the eggs with their stuffed side down on the toast, pour the sauce (see page 24) over the eggs and grill until the sauce bubbles.

Try the same dish with different sauces: the *Aïllade*, the *Pesto* or the *Garlic Cream* (see page 29).

POACHED EGGS ON TOMATO TOAST
WITH CHEESE SAUCE

Slice the bread and let it soak in the *Tomato Sauce* (see page 140), then place the bread slices in a hot oven for 10 minutes to get crisp. Poach an egg for each person, place one on each piece of crisp bread, cover them with a light *Cheese Sauce* (see page 28) and slip them under a hot grill for a moment.

HARICOT BEAN PURÉE WITH CHEESE

Spread the *Haricot Purée with Caraway* (see page 33) on toast, cover it liberally with grated Sage Derby cheese and place it under a hot grill until the cheese melts. Any of the dried bean *purées* can be used in this way.

TOASTED OLIVES AND MUSHROOMS

Slice ½ lb (225 g) of raw mushrooms thinly, pile them uncooked on the toast and cover them with the *Purée of Olives* (see page 39). Sprinkle them with Double Gloucester cheese and grill them.

Of course, the mushrooms could be lightly *sautéed* in butter first, but I prefer them almost raw beneath the hot cheese and the *Olive Purée*.

GARLIC CREAM TOAST

Beat 2 eggs into ¼ pint (150 ml) of *Garlic Cream* (see page 29), lay slices of bread in this mixture and leave them for 30 minutes, turning the slices so that both sides are coated. Cover each slice with breadcrumbs and fry them in hot oil.

As a supper dish, the bread can be served with one of the salads and the *Panais à la Provençale* (see page 193). As an appetizer, cut the bread into fingers before soaking it in the egg and the *Garlic Cream*.

BEAN PURÉES WITH EGG

To a large breakfastcup of any of the dried bean *purées* (see pages 33–6), add 2 beaten eggs and spread the mixture on toast. Then put the slices of toast under the grill until the egg has coagulated and the top is crisp and brown.

MUSHROOM PURÉE WITH EGG

Here again, add 2 beaten eggs to a large breakfastcup of *Mushroom Purée* (see page 39) or beat in more eggs and treat the mixture as scrambled. Serve it on toast or with fried garlic bread and sprinkle the egg and mushroom mixture with plenty of chopped parsley.

ARTICHOKE TOAST

Spread the *Artichoke Pâté* (see page 40) on toast and grill it until it begins to bubble and to brown slightly.

EGGS WITH WATERCRESS SAUCE

Boil several eggs, slice them when they are still warm and arrange them on pieces of toast. Pour over them the *Watercress and Egg Sauce* (see page 24) and place them under a hot grill.

FALAFELS

In Egypt (where they are called *ta'amia*), these are made from dried white broad beans. In Israel, they are made with chick peas. Nutty and heavily-spiced, they are good to eat as an appetizer or with *crudités* and a *purée* as an *hors d'oeuvre*, when they should be served hot or warm. Either yeast or baking powder can be used as a raising agent.

8 oz (225 g) dried chick peas or dried white broad beans
½ tsp baking powder or dry yeast
sugar
2 finely chopped large onions
2 crushed cloves of garlic
2 tsp each of ground coriander, fennel, aniseed and caraway
1 bunch finely chopped fresh parsley
salt and pepper
vegetable oil for shallow frying

Soak the dried pulses for an hour, changing the water three times, as described on page 32. After cooking, drain them and mince or liquidize to make a paste. If using yeast, prove it with a bit of sugar, dissolving both in a dessertspoon of warm water. Add this (once it has proved) and the remaining ingredients (except the oil) to the pulses and mix well. The mixture will be a bit more liquid if yeast is used, rather than baking powder, but don't worry. Let it stand for an hour in a warm place if you are using yeast or in the refrigerator if using baking powder. Then, with the fingers, take small bits of the mixture and mould them into little cakes. I flour them before dropping them into hot oil, as they tend to be sticky. If the paste seems too liquid to form into cakes or if you find that they disintegrate when put into the oil, take them from the pan, mix them again and add a couple of eggs. If you wish to make them lighter, fold 2 whipped egg whites into the mixture. I like the paradox of the earthy pulses aerated by the foam of the egg. Best warm, they can also be eaten cold, dipped into mayonnaise. This gives the same dissonance of earth and light.

1 **Parsnip and Caraway Falafels**
Boil 1 lb (450 g) of parsnips and mash them to a pulp, taking out any fibres that may have been in the centre. It is best, in fact, if the parsnips look large and weatherbeaten, not to cook the centre at all. Grind a good heaped tablespoon of caraway seeds in a mortar, then add these with salt and pepper to the parsnips with 1 oz (25 g) of butter and a tablespoon of thick cream. Fold in 2 whipped egg whites, 1 egg yolk and 4 oz (100 g) of breadcrumbs, and leave them in the refrigerator for a day. Proceed as for the *Falafels* above for the final cooking.

POTATO AND SESAME FALAFELS

Have 1 lb (450 g) of mashed potato. Bake 2 tablespoons of sesame seeds in the oven until they are brown. (A quicker way is to place them in a saucepan over a low heat, where they will start hopping about, but they are liable to burn this way unless watched constantly.)

Mix the sesame seeds into the mashed potato and season it well, then stir in an egg yolk. Lastly, beat in 2 whipped egg whites and place the mixture into the refrigerator to cool.

When you are ready to cook the *falafels*, pat spoonfuls of the mixture into ovals or spheres, then cook them in hot oil until they are crisp and brown on the outside.

These make a good appetizer and are also delicious piled up in a dish and served with an *Aïllade*, *Pesto* or hot *Tomato Sauce* (see pages 29 and 140) as a supper dish.

POTATO LATKES

1 lb (450 g) potatoes
2 large onions
2 beaten eggs
2 tbsp fine matzo meal
½ tsp baking powder
salt and pepper
vegetable oil for shallow frying

Peel and grate the potatoes into a bowl. Grate the onions and mix them with the potatoes. Add the eggs, matzo meal, baking powder and seasoning. Heat the oil until hot in a frying pan and drop spoonfuls of the mixture on to the oil. Fry until golden brown on both sides.

CROÛTES

Cut a French loaf into slices 1 inch thick. Then, using a grapefruit knife, cut a well from the centre of each slice about half an inch deep. With your fingers, press the bottom of the well towards the base of the bread, and do the same pressing, but outwards, to the sides. Brush the tops of the *croûtes* with melted butter and brown them in a hot oven for 5 minutes.

Have ready whatever filling you have decided on – the *Gruyère Fondue* (see page 88) or the cream cheese mixture on page 92, or some of the sauces, such as the mushroom or the tomato ones on pages 39 and 140. *Croûtes* can take any filling, hot or cold.

TURNOVERS

Roll out some short-crust pastry so that it is thin. Cut it into squares, ovals or circles. If making appetizers, these would be small, while for turnovers to eat as a supper dish, the circles would be larger and would emerge, when filled and sealed, more the size of a Cornish pastie.

On each piece of pastry, put a filling, using either the cream cheese mixture or the Stilton one on pages 91–2. Cover the filling, by either moistening the edges of the pastry with beaten egg, folding the pastry over and sealing it, or by simply putting another piece of pastry over the top of the first one.

Bake these in a hot oven until they puff up and are golden brown.

POIREAUX EN CROÛTE

enough short-crust pastry for a large double-crust pie
2 lb (1 kg) leeks
2 oz (50 g) butter
2 oz (50 g) flour
½ pt (300 ml) single cream
6 oz (175 g) grated Gruyère or cream cheese
salt and pepper
1 beaten egg

Clean the leeks after cutting them lengthways into quarters and discarding the more fibrous green leaves. Roll the pastry into a rectangle. Lay the leeks on the pastry, top to tail, like sardines. Put the pastry with the leeks into a buttered fireproof dish or a baking tin. Make a *roux* with the butter and the flour. Let it cook gently for a few minutes, then add the cream, slowly. When it is hot and smooth, stir in the cheese away from the heat, and season it with salt and pepper. This will make a thick, rich sauce; let it cool so that it is easier to handle.

Now spoon the sauce over the leeks, then fold both ends of the pastry up over the leeks. Brush the ends with the egg, then fold over the two remaining sides and pinch the pastry together. Bake in a hot oven for 30 minutes or until the pastry is cooked and brown. The leeks will exude some of their juices, which will mix and thin the sauce. Serve, garnished with sprigs of parsley.

STUFFED PRUNES

Take large prunes, soak them, cook until just tender, then leave them to drain. Stone them by cutting each prune in half. Fill each half with a mixture of cream cheese, a little grated Parmesan and some finely chopped fresh herbs – chives, parsley or mint. Sprinkle each one with paprika.

BAKED TIANS

As so many dishes take their names from the cooking utensil used for them, I have invented this name for a type of tart or *quiche* that is made without pastry. The nearest equivalent in French cooking are the *gratinée* dishes, but these often use ham or fish. Their advantage is that they are lighter and, of course, less fattening, but in order for them to be cut like a tart, they do need a *roux* base. There are endless variations, and I shall give only a few. Served with a fresh salad, they make an excellent supper.

EGG AND LEEK TIAN

1 lb (450 g) leeks
2 oz (50 g) butter
1 oz (25 g) flour
½ pt (300 ml) single cream
salt and pepper
4 beaten eggs
4 oz (100 g) Cheddar, Gruyère or cream cheese

Wash and chop the leeks, *sauté* them in a closed pan in the butter for 10–15 minutes, then work in the flour. When it has cooked through, take the leeks away from the heat and add the cream, stirring all the time so that the sauce begins to thicken. Season.

Butter a *tian*. Add the eggs to the leek mixture. Pour everything into the *tian* and sprinkle the cheese over the top, if using the Cheddar or Gruyère. Dot the cream cheese in blobs over the top otherwise; this cheese makes a lighter dish. The Gruyère will also melt into the sauce, while the Cheddar will go crispy. Put the dish into a preheated 350°F/180°C/Gas Mark 4 oven for 35–40 minutes.

You can sprinkle the dish before cooking with breadcrumbs
or add a little nutmeg to the sauce when making it. Like
quiches, tians should not be served at once; leave them for 5
minutes after they finish cooking so that they settle a bit. They
can then be cut and served more easily.

ONION AND CHEESE TIAN

3 large sliced onions
3 oz (75 g) butter
5 oz (150 g) Gruyère
5 oz (150 g) Cheddar or Sage Derby cheese
2 oz (50 g) flour
1 tsp caraway seeds
3 eggs
1 carton sour cream
salt and pepper

Sauté the onions in the butter until they are soft, about 8
minutes. Grate all the cheese and mix it with the flour. Butter
the *tian* and place half of the cheese at the bottom. Pour the
onions over the top. Crush the caraway seeds, add them to
the eggs, beat the mixture into the sour cream, season it and
pour it over the onions. Sprinkle the rest of the cheese on top.
Bake it in a preheated 350°F/180°C/Gas Mark 4 oven for about
35 minutes or until the top has risen and browned.

TOMATO AND ONION TIAN

1 14-oz (397-g) tin of tomatoes
2 large sliced onions
10 crushed cloves of garlic
2 oz (50 g) butter
2 oz (50 g) flour
1 glass red wine
1 tbsp tomato *purée*
1 tbsp dried basil
4 eggs
1 carton sour cream
salt and pepper
breadcrumbs
chopped parsley

Sauté the onions in the butter until soft. Drain the tomatoes and blend them into a *purée* with the garlic and the red wine. Put the tomatoes into a pan with the *purée* and the basil, and let them simmer for 5 minutes. Add the flour to the onions to thicken the juices, then add the tomato sauce to the onions and stir well, so that the sauce thickens smoothly. Take the sauce from the heat and beat in the eggs and the sour cream. Season, then pour it into a buttered *tian*, sprinkle the top with breadcrumbs and bake for 35 minutes. Sprinkle with the parsley and serve.

CHAPTER X

The Sacred Herb

People are either addicted to or fanatically against *Allium sativum*, the garlic we eat raw or use in cooking. Such is its strange potency, that it has inspired strong feelings throughout history. I make no apology for this chapter, which takes a quick glance at the history of a bulb whose essence can imbue so many different dishes with a singular perfection. Also, I am repaying a debt to it for the satisfaction it has given me, as well as celebrating its efficacy and invaluable aid to our health. And, too, it is a plea for understanding, so that those who find the cloves repugnant might be tempted to try large quantities of them cooked and so discover that their stringency has been miraculously changed into another quite different but wholly unique flavour which leaves no odour upon the breath whatsoever.

W. Keble Martin, in *The Concise British Flora*,* lists seven different species of wild garlic growing in the British Isles under the genus *Allium*. Two of these, *A. ursinum* (commonly referred to as wood garlic) and *A. oleraceum* (field garlic) have roots more in the nature of a spring onion and have not yet been cultivated into a cluster of cloves. Their flowers, white or pale cream, resemble the *Agapanthus*, for they are all related to the Liliaceae group (which includes lily of the valley and the wild leek as well as the whole range of exotic flowering bulbs that we know as lilies). It is perhaps not odd that the plant which produces such a unique flavour belongs to a botanical family containing species which flower into equally distinctive beauty and produce the most fragrant scent of all blooms.

Though several varieties of wild garlic are becoming rare, *A. triquetrum* has become naturalized in isolated parts of

* *The Concise British Flora*, W. Keble Martin, Ebury Press and Michael Joseph.

south-west England. It spreads freely, grows to a foot in height and flowers in clusters of greenish-white stars. Most varieties of wild garlic smell distinctively, though far less pungently, of the bulb we use in cooking. However, you would not find them except in distant rural areas or on the banks of the canal system, where most varieties of wild flowers and herbs still flourish happily.

The plant is thought to have originated in south-western Siberia, which at that time must have been tropical, for garlic flourishes in the sun and needs a well-drained loamy soil (though I have seen it on many Mediterranean islands growing happily from what seemed like a thin layer of grit).

In Old English, garlic was garleac, its derivation coming from the French *gar* (spear) and the Old English leac (leek). Until the first third of the fifteenth century, it was also a name for a jig or a farce, both being a source of laughter and entertainment. The use of this term for such a performance indicates an awareness that the root had other properties which were in some sense magical.

Superstitious myths have always surrounded the bulb and reach back into history as far as ancient Egypt. Inside the Cheops pyramid at Giza, Herodotus found an inscription telling of the vast number of garlics, onions and radishes eaten by the labourers while building the pyramid. Garlic was obviously highly esteemed, as it was used as currency. The arrangement of the cloves in a crude cosmic parallel (in that they rotate around a central core) and the bulb's medicinal qualities also gave it a magical aura, so that it was used by people for swearing oaths.

From Egypt on to Greece and Rome, where an atmosphere both reverential and obscene surrounded the eating of it. This adds to its mystery; it is as if some people were frightened of the bulb, while others nervously made coarse jokes about it. Circe feared it: Homer recounts how Ulysses escaped from her by plucking up a plant and waving it in her face.

In Roman times, Pliny lists all manner of bizarre ingredients for love potions and erotic stimulants. They nearly always include an onion and sometimes garlic; about the only edible objects among moon-head beetles, dung from dog-headed apes, gum and myrtle resin. The relationship between a love potion and an object to protect the wearer from the evil eye is close, for the baneful influence which people feared was the loss of sexual potency.

In Rome, Suetonius tells an anecdote about the Emperor Vespasian. 'To let slip no opportunity of improving military discipline, when a young man reeking with perfumes came to thank him for a commission which had been given him, Vespasian drew back his head in disgust, adding the stern reprimand: "I would rather you had smelt of garlic".'* And then he revoked the commission.

Then, as now, the sacred bulb seems to have attracted extreme feelings. Horace devoted the whole of this third *Epode* to 'The Wicked Garlic' and began with a dour warning: 'If ever any man with impious hand strangle an aged parent, may he eat of garlic, deadlier than the hemlock'. Virgil, on the other hand, was far more balanced and reasonable, and in the poem, *Moretum*, in the *Appendix Vergiliana* gives us a scene where the peasant farmer is obviously an epicure chef in embryo. 'At first, light digging up the ground with his fingers, he draws out four garlic bulbs with thick fibres,† then plucks slender parsley leaves and unbending rue, and coriander, trembling on its scanty stalk.' Later: ' . . . he first crushes with a pestle the fragrant garlic, then grinds all evenly in a juicy mixture'.

In the Dark Ages, the myth that the bulbs could ward off the evil eye deepened still further, and from here its use in the Count Dracula legend might have begun. That clusters of garlic with a crucifix were enough to terrify the vampire suggests that its ritual and religious associations were still strong.

In English literature, garlic is not often mentioned and when it is, it is often derogatory. Chaucer tells us of his Summoner: 'Wel loved he garleek, oynons and eek lekes'. That he was also hot and lecherous would support the myth that garlic is an aphrodisiac, but that the Summoner was covered in carbuncles negates the claim for the purgative properties of the bulb in this case. The hideous picture that Chaucer paints of this man – who appears to be in the terminal stages of venereal acne – would imply the author's dislike of his subject's profession perhaps more than his eating habits. Or, in the

* '*Maluissem alium oboluisses.*'
† '*Ac primum, leviter digitis tellure refossa/ quattor educit cum spissis alia fibris . . .*'

Summoner's case, he may well have come to the chewing of garlic late in life.

Hotspur claims, 'I had rather live with cheese and garlic in a windmill', than endure Glendower, who had a habit of spouting about Merlin. Hotspur was sensible, in that he preferred garlic to Glendower, but he obviously rated it as an inferior alternative. Also, it possibly suggests that in Shakespeare's mind the charlatan magician and the pungent bulb were not that far apart.

Charles Lamb disdains garlic, referring to it as 'guilty' in his *Essay on Roast Pig* (he refers to the sauce for this meat as being made with breadcrumbs mashed up with liver and the brains and a dash of mild sage) and is quite horrified that onions, shallots or the 'guilty garlic' should ever be used. However, even *they*, he says, cannot poison the flavour of pork. (This may explain the mental instability of his family, for recent experiments indicate that the onion family counteracts the high cholesterol effect of fatty meats.)

The English, in their pragmatic fashion, tend to disregard any ideas that a particular food is an aphrodisiac, so I cannot think that Charles Lamb thought garlic was 'guilty' on that score. Norman Douglas, in his charming satire on this idea, does not even bother to mention garlic in his many recipes. Yet any food or spice which is fiery to the taste and which seems to give the body a warm glow could well stimulate the erectile tissues, and it seems unreasonable for us to dismiss the ancients as naïve in this respect.

It disappoints me greatly that garlic is thought of with such distrust. In *French Country Cooking*, Elizabeth David quotes Ford Madox Ford and his story of the ravishing model who had cooked *Poulet Bérnais* with its requisite amount of garlic – 2 lb. ' . . . she had schooled her organs to assimilate, not to protest against, the sacred herb . . . ' How unlike Circe. The point of the story is that if you regularly eat large amounts of garlic, there is little offensive aroma to upset the unconverted. What is more, not only does the digestion improve, but also the body's general health. Another extraordinary fact is that when you use large quantities of garlic in cooking, the pungent aroma and flavour change into something unique, for it is almost subtle – still slightly indignant, but with the fiery essence suffused by the creamy consistency of the cloves. I have made a garlic soup with one hundred and twenty-five cloves, which made only enough for three people; but the interesting fact about it is that though highly delicious, it was not noticeably stronger than the same soup made from fifty cloves.

Rosemary Hemphill, in *Herbs for All Seasons*, says: 'Garlic has been known for centuries to contain antiseptic substances', and there follows a passage where she says it can lower high blood pressure, ward off colds, ease rheumatism and clear the complexion. She also mentions its use in World War I for sterilizing swabs to prevent wounds turning septic.*

Now that we are importing a new giant variety of garlic with each clove the size of a thumb, it is impossible to give exact amounts in recipes. Besides, flavouring with garlic depends upon personal taste. However, I would beg everyone to be bold about their generosity with this pungent bulb.

I have long felt that recipes using garlic are not adventurous enough, yet it is a powerful flavour and must not swamp a dish. Recipes made practically from garlic only are very few; we have the great *aïoli* (and its Greek counterpart, *skordalia*), garlic butter and *soupe à l'ail* from Provence and south-western France, but what else? We must return to Greece, where a variation upon their *avgolemono* sauce can be a stimulus to our imagination.

AVGOLÉMONO SAUCE

This Greek sauce is made from fish, meat or poultry stock, but the importance of it here is that it also uses garlic, lemon and egg yolks.

Beat the juice from a lemon with 3 egg yolks, then take $\frac{1}{4}$ pint (150 ml) of the liquid from under the *Garlic Cream* (see page 29) and heat it. Mix the liquid with the lemon and the egg yolks as you would have done for the soup on page 51. It is a perfect sauce for *oeufs mollets*.

---

* She also recommends it as a purgative for worms which the Egyptians were well aware of as they list that parasite among other ailments in their *Medical Papyrus* that dates from 1550 B.C. It claims that if given to dogs, it will expel the worms within twelve hours. My own dog, who has not suffered from worms, will eat garlic with enthusiasm – and it's not necessary to peel the cloves.

GARLIC BUTTER

¼ lb (225 g) salted butter
5 large cloves of garlic
juice from 2 lemons
black pepper

Squeeze the juice from the garlic, but discard the outer skins. Place the crushed garlic with the lemon juice in a small pan and poach it gently with the lid on for 10 minutes. This releases all the flavour of the garlic and avoids the harsh rawness which is another delight altogether.

Allow the butter to soften by leaving it at room temperature for a bit. When the lemon and garlic mixture has cooled, add it to the butter in a bowl and mix well. Put it into the refrigerator so that the butter will harden again. This method avoids the business of melting the butter and cooking the garlic in it, for then the finished dish has a layer of clarified butter on top, while the rest is soft and so cannot be spread.

When altering a French loaf into garlic bread, some people melt the butter with the garlic and pour it over a loaf which has been sliced almost to its base. I have found that this method does not get the garlic butter into the centre of the loaf, and that often more of the butter falls outside the loaf and on to the foil covering. It is far better to spread the butter on the inside of each slice and then to close the loaf up again by twisting the foil tightly.

AÏOLI

Use 1 large clove of garlic or 3–5 small ones and crush them before putting them into the blender with a little salt and black pepper. Blend the garlic with barely a teaspoon of lemon juice into a milky white paste, then add 2 egg yolks and blend it again, but gently, as too much agitation disturbs the yolks and too much lemon can curdle them before the oil is added. It is sometimes safer, if the garlic has been well crushed, to do this part of the operation in a bowl and to mix with a wooden spoon. Then proceed as you would for a pure mayonnaise, adding ¼ pint (150 ml) of oil or more, drop by drop to begin with. It is best to put the olive oil into a jug and to pour from that, as the steady stream can then be controlled.

SAUCE ROUILLE

10 green chillies
6 crushed cloves of garlic
salt
4 oz (100 g) breadcrumbs
¼ pt (150 ml) olive oil

Bake the chillies in a low oven for 45 minutes, so that they are dried. After they have cooled, break off the stalks and crumble the rest into a bowl. Add the garlic cloves, the salt and the breadcrumbs. Slowly pour in the olive oil, stirring it all the time.

Being a hot and somewhat fiery sauce, this is best with the blandest of dishes and is perfect with plainly steamed cauliflower or a cheese mousse.

BAKED POTATOES STUFFED WITH GARLIC

Make a *Garlic Soup* with 30 cloves of garlic (see page 51). Leave it to cool and do not blend it, for the stock can be strained from the cloves and kept for another soup. When the potatoes are baked, slice them in two, scoop the insides into a bowl, and add the cooked garlic cloves and enough of the stock to moisten the potato. Then place them under a hot grill to brown on top.

BAKED ONIONS STUFFED WITH GARLIC

Choose several large onions and allow one for each person. Cut off the tops and the bases. Then, with a grapefruit knife, hollow out the centres. Place the removed cores into a blender with about 20 cloves of garlic to 6 onions; add salt and pepper and 3 tablespoons of olive oil. Blend for a minute until it has become a creamy liquid. Fill the hollow in each onion with this *purée*.

Pour 1 tablespoon of olive oil into a casserole and add ¼ pint (150 ml) of boiling water. Place the onions into this and wedge them in tightly. Sprinkle each one with breadcrumbs and bake in the oven for 1 hour at a medium heat.

GARLIC RICE

Make the *Garlic Soup* as on page 51. Instead of liquidizing the soup add 6 oz (175 g) of uncooked rice at that point and bring it back to the boil. Simmer for 6 minutes on top of the stove or until the rice has soaked up all of the liquid. You can instead bake the rice in the oven as with a *risotto*, which is easier.

When the rice is cooked, stir it so that the garlic cloves are mixed with the grains and add some finely chopped parsley before serving.

GARLIC CABBAGE WITH EGGS

1 small white cabbage
finely chopped cloves from 1 head of garlic
1 tbsp vegetable oil
1 grated ginger root
1 tbsp *satay* or five-spice powder
salt and pepper
2 beaten eggs

Slice the cabbage thinly and peel the garlic by pouring water over the cloves. Stir-fry both (see page 116) in the oil for about 2 minutes or until the cabbage has lost half of its bulk. Add the ginger root and the *satay* or five-spice powder. Cook for another minute, stirring all the time. Season it with salt and pepper, then add the beaten eggs and scramble them into the vegetables, as with a *pipérade*. The cabbage should be *al dente*.

POTATO AND GARLIC FALAFELS

Have 1 lb (450 g) of well-mashed potato that has been seasoned with sea salt and black pepper. While it is still warm, squeeze into it the juice and skins from a dozen cloves of crushed garlic and mix well. Add an egg to bind and leave the mixture to cool in the refrigerator for an hour. Then roll the mixture with your fingers into balls the size of a walnut and cover them in breadcrumbs. Shallow fry them in olive oil in a hot pan until they are brown and crisp on the outside. If you use the *Garlic Cream* (see page 29), the flavour is so subtle that it is hardly noticeable. The rather heavy quality of the potato takes to the raw garlic much better.

ROASTED GARLIC

A dish for the addicts, to be enjoyed hot; at table, some people mistake it for a dish of white haricot beans and then ask how one has made the beans taste so delicious. Peel enough cloves for your guests – 200 small cloves for six guests or about 4 heads of the large garlic. Toss the cloves of garlic in 2 tablespoons of olive oil and season them. Place them in a covered earthenware dish in a preheated oven for half an hour at a medium heat. Serve sprinkled with a little parsley.

Bread

The three bread recipes that follow use garlic and are easy to make as the dough is stirred and not kneaded. I believe we ought to be more adventurous in the flavourings used in home baking. The simplest dish – say, scrambled eggs – on a slice of toast from any of these breads is delicious. Or they can be baked before a dinner party and served warm with the *crudités* or soup.

HERB AND GARLIC BREAD

10 oz (275 g) wholemeal flour
4 tsp dry yeast
1½ tbsp black molasses
1 tsp salt
4 fl oz (100 ml) water
4 fl oz (100 ml) milk
1 oz (25 g) butter
2 oz (50 g) grated onion
5 crushed cloves of garlic
1 tsp crushed rosemary
1 tsp dill seed
1 tsp thyme

Mix the dry yeast, the molasses and the warm water together; leave it to allow the yeast to ferment. Melt the butter in the milk with the salt. Add the crushed herbs, garlic cloves and grated onion to the yeast with the flour and the milk. Stir with a wooden spoon until all the ingredients are well mixed. Cover the bowl with a cloth and leave it in a warm place until the dough has risen. When it has tripled its bulk, stir it again and tip it into a greased bread tin. Let it stand until the dough has risen to the top of the tin. Place in a preheated 350°F/180°C/Gas Mark 4 oven for an hour.

1   **Baked Garlic Loaf**
    10 oz (275 g) white flour (or an equal mixture of white and
       wholemeal flour)
    8 fl oz (225 ml) *Garlic Soup* (see page 51)
    1 oz (25 g) butter
    4 tsp dry yeast
    1½ tbsp honey

Heat the soup and in it melt the butter and dissolve the
salt. Put it to one side. Mix the yeast with the honey and
3 tablespoons of the warm soup to start the yeast fermenting.
Leave it for a few minutes or until the bubbles are rising
to the surface. Then add the flour and the rest of the soup.
Stir well. When the mixture is smooth proceed as for the
Herb and Garlic Bread above. The flavour is delicate, yet
positive, unlike the next recipe where it is dominant and
pungent.

2   **Spiced Bread**
    10 oz (275 g) wholemeal flour
    8 dsp milk
    1 oz (25 g) butter
    1 tsp salt
    4 tsp dry yeast
    1½ tbsp sugar
    8 dsp water
    2 tbsp curry spices (see page 25)
    10 crushed cloves of garlic

Heat the milk and in it melt the butter and dissolve the
salt. Ferment the yeast with the sugar in the water; the
last should be warm enough to start the yeast working.
Mix the spices and the garlic with the flour. Add this to
the yeast mixture and proceed as for the *Herb and Garlic
Bread*.

Index to Recipes

Index

cabbage, white—*continued*
  cabbage tarkari, 178
  carrot, apple and cabbage salad, 112–13
  garlic cabbage with eggs, 217
  paprika cabbage, 188
  potage de chou aïllade, 50
  stuffed cabbage, 167–70
caraway, *32*
  baked potatoes stuffed with parsnip and
    caraway, 160
  haricot bean purée with caraway, 33–4
  parsnip and caraway falafels, 204
cardamom, *71*
carrots
  aubergine and carrot mousse, 102–3
  carrot, apple and cabbage salad, 112–13
  carrot puffs, 186
  carrot and radish purée, 42
  carrot soup, 53
  carrots with cream, 186
  carrots with marsala, 187
  glazed carrots, 186
  new carrots, 185
  pesto soup, 52
  raw carrots, 17
casein, *31*
cauliflower
  baked vegetables with yoghurt paste,
    179
  cauliflower cheese, 175–6
  cauliflower pilau, 125
  cauliflower purée, 41
  cauliflower salad, 109
  cream of cauliflower soup, 52–3
  raw cauliflower, 17
celery
  celery and nasturtium leaves salad, 109
  celery soup, 56
  fennel and celery salad, 112
celestial soup, 54
Cheddar cheese, *70, 71*
cheese, *70–1*
  artichokes with ginger and cheese, 180
  baked rigatoni with cream cheese, 141
  cauliflower cheese, 175–6
  cheese and mushroom pancakes, 165
  cheese omelette, 79
  cheese pancakes with sauce moutarde, 165
  cheese sandwich croûtons, 90
  cheese sauce, 28 (sauce mornay), 73
  cheese soufflé, 93–5
  cheese spread, 92
  cream cheese gnocchi, 143
  cream cheese omelette, 79
  fondue croquettes, 89–90
  fried cheese, 90
  fried cheese and egg sandwich, 91
  gnocchi baked with cheese, 145
  Gruyère cheese fondue, 88–9, 146
  haricot bean purée with cheese, 202
  leek and Sage Derby soup, 60

macaroni cheese, 138
melted cheese on toast, 91
onion and cheese tian, 208
pasta with cream cheese, 141–2
poached eggs on tomato toast with
  cheese sauce, 202
purée of potatoes with cream cheese, 156
soft herb cheese, 92
Stilton cheese balls, 91–2
Welsh rarebit, 91
see also mousses; quiches; soufflés
Cheshire cheese, *70(2)*
chestnuts
  brussels sprout and chestnut soup, 61
  red cabbage with chestnuts, 188
  walnut and chestnut sauce, 22–3
chick peas
  falafels, 203–5
  hummus, 35–6
chicory, 194
  with cream sauce, 195
  raw, 17–18
chillies
  chilli eggs, 84
  chilli sauce, 73–4
  chilli soup, 66
  purée of green peas and chilli, 34–5
  sauce rouille, 216
Chinese beans, 35
Chinese risotto, 133
Chinese salads, 115–20
Chinese soups, 54–5
chives
  cucumber and chive salad, 111
chou farci provençale, 168
coconut, cabbage with, 179
cold marinade, marinating, 116
  cold marinated marrow, 197–8
coriander, *71*
  cabbage and coriander soup, 61
courgettes, 183
  courgette and parsley soup, 64
  courgettes in sweet and sour sauce, 184
  fried courgettes, 184
  Italian fried courgettes, 184
  ratatouille, 180–1
cream
  baked cucumbers with cream sauce, 183
  carrots with cream, 186
  cucumber and cream sauce, 147
  new potatoes with cream sauce, 154
  parsnips with mushrooms and cream,
    193
  sauce à la crème, 24
  scrambled eggs with onion and sour
    cream, 77
  spinach with cream, 185
crêpes, *see* pancakes
croquettes
  fondue croquettes, 89–90
  parsnip croquettes, 194

222

Index of Persons

Acton, Eliza, 182
Austen, Jane, 69

Beck, Simone, and others, 28n.
Blount, Sir Thomas, 31
Boulestin, Marcel, 70
Brahms, Caryl, and S. J. Simon, 160n.

Chaucer, Geoffrey, 212–13
Columbié, Auguste, 31

David, Elizabeth, 23, 25n., 31, 81, 126, 213
Disraeli, Benjamin, 69
Douglas, Norman, 213

Ford, Ford Madox, 213

Grigson, Jane, 193

Hartley, Dorothy, 83
Hemphill, Rosemary, 32, 214
Herodotus, 211
Homer, 211
Horace, 212

Lamb, Charles, 213

Martin, W. Keble, 210

Pliny, 211

Shakespeare, William, 213
Suetonius, 212

Virgil, 212